AVAILABLE TITLES

THE WHY BLUEPRINT

Copyright © 2023 by Dr. Y. Bur. All rights reserved.

Visit www.RoarPublishingGroup.com for more information. No part of this publication may be reproduced, stored in a retrieval system, or transmitted in any way by any means, electronic, mechanical, photocopy, recording, or otherwise, without the prior permission of the author except as provided by USA copyright law.

Book design copyright © 2023 by R.O.A.R. International Group. All rights reserved.

R.O.A.R. Publishing Group
581 N. Park Ave. Ste. #725
Apopka, FL 32704
ROAR-58-2316
762-758-2316
www.RoarPublishingGroup.com
DrYBur@gmail.com

Published in the United States of America
ISBN: 978-1-948936-74-3
$22.88

Send *As It Pleases God*®
Book Series **and** *Workbook* **Testimonies, Donations, Questions, or Orders to:**

Dr. Y. Bur
R.O.A.R. Publishing Group
581 N. Park Ave. Ste. #725
Apopka, FL 32704
ROAR~58~2316
762~758~2316

📧 Dr.YBur@gmail.com

Visit Us At:
 AsItPleasesGodMovement
▶ AsItPleasesGod

🖥 DrYBur.com
🖥  AsItPleasesGod.com

Please Donate

Please DONATE to this *Missionable Movement of God* as a GIVE-BACK to the Kingdom. Thanks for your support. Many Blessings.

AIPG Donation Link
Custom Amount

Scan to Pay

Table of Contents

Introduction 9
Chapter One 15
  Rules to the Game 15
    Pitfalls of Omission 19
Chapter Two 25
  The Wise Blueprint 25
    Purposeful Intents 28
    Allow Wisdom to Speak 30
Chapter Three 37
  H.O.M.E. Base 37
    My Seed, My Root, and My Fruit 42
Chapter Four 49
  The WHY Blueprint 49
    Self-Questions 55
    Building Character 59
    Spiritual Reflective Measures 78
    Divine Inclusion 84
Chapter Five 89
  Blueprint Hindrances 89
    Proud Look 90

Lying Tongue...92
  Innocent Blood...94
  Devises Wicked Plans..98
  Running To Evil..101
  False Witness...107
  Sowing Discord..113
Chapter Six..117
  Fresh Oil..117
Chapter Seven..125
  Reverse Engineer...125
Chapter Eight..133
  The SEEDED Mindset..133
Chapter Nine...141
  Closing the Divide..141
    The Belt of Truth..146
    The Breastplate of Righteousness.......................149
    The Shoes of the Gospel of Peace......................155
    The Shield of Faith..161
    The Helmet of Salvation......................................173
    The Sword of The Spirit.......................................188
    The Whole Armor of God...................................191
Chapter Ten...195
  Overcoming Insecurity...195

Kingdom Confidence 206
Chapter Eleven 209
　The Lord Will Provide 209
　　Divine Communication 214
　　The Contingency Clause 224
Chapter Twelve 227
　Doctoring The WHY 227

INTRODUCTION

Why do you exist? What do you need to achieve? What is your purpose? How can you make a difference? What is the legacy you want to leave behind? These are some of the questions everyone asks themselves, especially during uncertainty, confusion, or loss. For this reason, a straightforward guide can help us with decision-making, aligning our actions, understanding our journey, and how to self-correct, redirect, and reapproach, *As It Pleases God*.

Today's most prominent element of confusion is between Divine Purpose and average purpose. Our Divine Purpose is why we exist, beyond making money or providing a service. A self-made purpose is about making money, gaining power, status, fame, fortune, and recognition without tapping into the Spiritual Aspects of who we are.

The WHY Blueprint aims to bring you in Purpose on purpose. If you desire power, status, fame, and fortune without tapping into your reason for being, this book is NOT for you.

Why? The ultimate purpose is to put your Spirit Man into business with what you already possess from within. With this *Spirit to Spirit* and *Spirit to Business* approach, you must possess the MINDSET and MOTIVES that can break strongholds, yokes, and blockages. If not, you will become drawn away, distracted, or detoured easily.

The WHY Blueprint is a strategic method of merging our performance and impact toward fulfilling our Predestined Purpose. Balancing our Mental, Physical, Emotional, and Spiritual Scales, *As It Pleases God*, helps us articulate and document our purpose, vision, mission, values, goals, and action plans.

In the Eye of God, we must learn how to MASTER *The Rules of the Game* when dealing with the Vicissitudes, Cycles, and Seasons of life. If not, we can become victims watching everyone pass by, doing their thing without us knowing what to do, why, or how. With this book, I will lay out *The WHY Blueprint*, but it will be left up to you to put in the work, Spiritually Tilling your own ground. If you skip steps, you are accountable if you misstep, misunderstand, misread, or get mixed up.

As life would have it, imbalance has become a focal point of our feelings associated with Purpose Jilting. When we secretly or openly feel jilted, the psyche rebels against the surrounding people, places, and things associated with us. For example, we are Spiritually Grounded but lack the business savvy to bring our Divine Purpose to life. Or, we are well-grounded in doing business and making a lot of money, but we are Spiritually Aloof or lack business integrity. According to the Heavenly of Heavens, we can have all the above in the Eye of God if we lay out the BLUEPRINT, *As It Pleases Him*.

We are a right now generation, and doing business God's way is not always our top priority. Thus, according to the Heavenly of Heavens, to maximize our Gifts, Calling, Talents, and Creativity, there is a Divine Order attached. For example, we cannot become a writer with nothing to say. The words, thoughts, visions, desires, beliefs, or stories must flow from somewhere, and that somewhere is from within.

With *The WHY Blueprint*, we will discuss tapping into what is already within, using Spiritual Principles, Tools, and Metaphors with relevant business strategies. Putting the WHY behind what we do helps us build, maintain, sustain, and harvest the fruits of our labor, making all the difference in the world.

The WHY Blueprint combines Spirituality with our Predestined Purpose, linking the Business Knowledge needed to make it work, *As It Pleases God*. It is a powerful tool, helping us achieve our goals and improve our performance, Mentally, Physically, Emotionally, and Spiritually, leaving no stone unturned.

The Wise Blueprint wants to help us in *Closing the Divide* between our past, present, and future. It is done by helping us to:

- ☐ Clarify and Communicate.
- ☐ Align and Engage.
- ☐ Focus and Prioritize.
- ☐ Monitor and Improve.
- ☐ Celebrate and Share.

In the Kingdom of God, our Divine Purpose or Predestined Blueprint is the epiphany of expectancy. Being we are all different, *The WHY Blueprint* is not a rigid or static framework like a one-shoe-fits-all approach. It is flexible with the agility to adapt to the differences of all who participate wholeheartedly, especially when connecting to our H.O.M.E. Base.

Connecting the Dots in our lives is not always easy, especially if we do not know what to do or why we are doing it. Therefore, we must develop *The SEEDED Mindset* of planting, sowing, regrafting, and sharing, allowing the Seedtime and Harvest Principle to help us, our Divine Blueprint, and our Bloodline.

When we are *Branded and Highly Favored*, the only limits we have are the ones we place on ourselves. Regardless of where we are or what we have going on, we are uniquely purposed for something with Spiritual Access to everything attached to what we are predestined to do. What does this mean? We have Divine Provisions attached to our Predestined Blueprint. However, we must focus on *Overcoming Insecurities* that keep us from stepping out of our comfort zones, especially when *Doing Business*.

The *Passionate Persuasion* of moving the Heart of God is to grow and develop, *As It Pleases Him*. Of course, we are not robots, but if we willfully focus on faith and obedience, doing what He has called us to do, it will change the trajectory of our lives.

Some do not have time to change their lives and expect Supernatural Results without planning for excellence. With *The WHY Blueprint*, we put in the work! I call it *Doctoring the WHY*, but you can call it the ANSWER. Here is what you can glean from *The WHY Blueprint*:

- ☐ You will learn the *Rules of the Game*.
- ☐ You will become well-versed in understanding and addressing the *Pitfalls of Omission*.

- ☐ You will understand the value of *exercising wisdom* on a moment-by-moment basis.
- ☐ You will be able to MASTER your own WHY Blueprint.
- ☐ You will understand the secrets of suiting up with the *Whole Armor of God*.
- ☐ You will be able to CONNECT your own unique dots.
- ☐ You will get an understanding of your BRANDED style from the inside out.
- ☐ You will become comfortable with who you are and what you were born to do.
- ☐ You will learn how to create a Blueprint, Mind Map, or Road Map for your life, business, or Divine Purpose.
- ☐ You will learn the value of *Kingdom Communication*.

So, if you are ready to understand the WHY behind you, then let us pull back the Divine VEIL on the GREATNESS already residing within you. Yes, you!

CHAPTER ONE
Rules to the Game

Let us begin this book with my infamous quote, '*Life is a game, you play, or you be played, but if you play by the MASTER'S RULES, you will win every time.*' This quote caused mayhem in my life, provoking the naysayers to prove God a liar, make me out of one, bring shame to my name, or thwart my Divine Mission. Yet, here we are...proving God will not be mocked, nor shall we take His NAME in vain.

Can you imagine contending with God Almighty as a human being? Is it even possible to be more powerful than God, the Divine Creator of all things? How is it that we play with the lives of others without accounting for the seeds, deeds, and weeds sown? Will they not bring life in due season? The *Rules to the Game* are written on the tablet of our hearts, and if we fail to read them or override them for selfish reasons, we will 'get got' by what we set in motion with a mirrored effect.

If we decide to play a game, there are rules attached. So, why are we living without them, doing, saying, and becoming whatever to please ourselves? Do we not have the right to play by our own rules? Absolutely. We are free-will agents. We can do, say, and become whatever, whenever, and however, but when it is time to clean up our mess, we may run into a brick wall. Why? We did not play by the rules, *As It Pleases God*. Yes, we do have grace and mercy working on our behalf, but there are consequences and repercussions for unruliness.

The *Rules to the Game* should begin with, *As It Pleases God*. If it begins with 'as it pleases ourselves,' we change the game's trajectory. Why would this happen? In due time, we will turn on ourselves because we are not designed to place ourselves above God Almighty. More importantly, if we defy our Divine Blueprint or fail to make an effort to know what it is, we create a Spiritual Void for ourselves.

What is a Spiritual Void? The emptiness felt from within contributes to the negative inner chatter and secret insecurities. What if we do not have insecurities or do not speak negatively to ourselves? Unfortunately, we are all created with a void, and we will all naturally speak negatively or lie unless we are taught otherwise. In the carnality of it all, when someone comes to me with this foolery, I already know what and who I am dealing with.

The Game of Life is nothing to joke around with. It has seasons, cycles, and vicissitudes designed to train us into Divine Formation. If we decide on rebellion to become our portion, we will find our thoughts, emotions, desires, and biases becoming ruthless and selfish beyond reasoning. If one does not believe this, take a loving couple, building a life together, and then one person decides to divorce the relationship. We will find them becoming archenemies, who once thought they loved each other. How can this be? It was conditional! Once the condition was no longer satisfying a need, their true colors were unveiled. In essence, they did not just become that person instantly; it was under layers of something else.

For me, I do not look at how a person behaves in the good times; I want to see how they handle the bad. To be clear, I do not wish ill will upon anyone; however, I want to see how they handle pressure, chaos, confusion, rejection, and so on. Anyone can put on a show, but when they do not get what they want, will they throw a book across the room? Will they cause harm to another person's property or damage their own due to their lack of self-control? This behavior is not cute when dealing with *The Rules of the Game*. For this reason, *The WHY Blueprint* cuts to the chase. We want to know the seed, root, and fruit of the WHAT and WHY. By not knowing this, we can become our worst enemy while pretending to be our best friend.

Whether we play by the rules or know nothing about our Divine Blueprint, it does not give us an excuse to avoid learning about charactorial development and using our people skills. What is the purpose of charactorial development and using our people skills? Once we get into the room or achieve our goals and desires, we want them to remain. Unfortunately, the lack of charactorial development and our people skills keep us out of the room or get us booted out, causing underlying victimization, insecurity, trauma, or rebellion.

A lot of people are trained to talk a good game, but if our thoughts, actions, reactions, biases, and lack of self-control are our downfall, then how good is our game, right? According to the Heavenly of Heavens, the ideal mindset is to be it, own it, and share it. We do not have to brag, boast, or roast, especially when we can handle our business, *As It Pleases God*. Our lives or whatever will speak for themselves, period. No convincing is necessary.

On the other hand, if we find ourselves convincing others about our game, it means our game is NOT tight, right, or there is some spite going on. We must check our Spiritual Fruits to ensure envy, jealousy, greed, pride, coveting, and competitiveness are not coming from us. Why must we check for these items? If they come from us, they cannot become our fuel, leverage, propellant, or stepping stone. If it comes from the opposing force, it must provide us with fuel, leverage, propellant, or a stepping stone because our Spiritual Fruits are right, tight, and on point. Clearly, this does not mean we will not be provoked or should not stand up for what is right; we must learn how to ask the right questions amid provocation.

According to the Heavenly of Heavens, it takes a negative and a positive, or a positive to positive, to produce Spiritual Power. Thus, a negative on negative is DEADWEIGHT unless converted by a positive. Above all, we need positive seeds, roots, vines, and fruits; whatever is negative must be pruned. Although the negative can build, empower, and strengthen us, we cannot allow it to hang around. We must make the necessary adjustments, learn, grow, and share while keeping it moving in the Spirit of Excellence. What makes this so important? When dealing with *The WHY Blueprint*, we do not want deadweight hanging around, dragging us down, or distracting us.

When we are on a Divine Mission or dealing with *The Rules of the Game*, although we operate with the Fruits of the Spirit and behave Christlike, we must limit our time with people, places, and things resistant to pruning, training, and improving. We must move to where we are needed, appreciated, and utilized without depriving them of the resources needed to make them better, stronger, and wiser for the Kingdom of God. Bottom line, we are just as accountable for wasting time as we are for where we spend it, how, and why.

Pitfalls of Omission

Have you ever experienced the feeling of someone intentionally omitting vital information from you? It can be frustrating, confusing, and even hurtful. You may wonder why they did not trust you enough to share the truth. Then again, you may feel betrayed, angry, or disappointed.

The overt act of intentionally or unintentionally leaving something out can become daunting for most who are blindsided by an ugly truth. On the other hand, omission can save time, avoid repeating known information, or whitewash the unknown to benefit those who know. For this reason, it is essential to be careful with what we omit; whitewashing can lead to confusion, misunderstanding, or trust issues, especially when doing Kingdom Business or planning for success, *As It Pleases God.*

What is the big deal about the *Pitfalls of Omission*? When dealing with *The WHY Blueprint*, omitting one item or issue can distort the plan. Why? Not planning for success, justifying our faults, and lying to ourselves or others are the common pitfalls among many individuals and businesses. If left unchecked, they will lead to missed opportunities, wasted resources, and ultimate failure.

While honesty and transparency are generally seen as positive traits, there may be some benefits to omission in certain situations. Here are a few potential benefits of omission:

- Protection of privacy: By omitting specific details, individuals can protect their own privacy and the privacy of others.

- Avoidance of harm: In some cases, omitting information can prevent harm to oneself or others.
- Simplification of communication: Omitting unnecessary information can simplify communication and make it easier to understand.

- Respect for boundaries: By not disclosing certain information, individuals can respect the boundaries of others and avoid overstepping them.

- Maintenance of confidentiality: Omitting sensitive information can help maintain confidentiality and prevent leaks.

- Preservation of relationships: Omitting information that may cause conflict or hurt feelings can help preserve relationships.

- Protection of trade secrets: In business, omitting specific details can help protect trade secrets and intellectual property.

The *Pitfalls of Omission* that I am referring to in this chapter are the NEED-TO-KNOW information, such as the intricate details, that have the potential to create entangled snares for ourselves or others. On the other hand, if we use omission as a form of manipulation to gain an advantage or control over someone or something, we change the *Rules of the Game* in the

Eye of God. Why are the rules changed? The *Pitfall of Omission* is a seed-bearing fruit.

Manipulative omission allows people to get into your head, making you feel less than others, thwarting your growth, downplaying your accomplishments, or invoking doubt. If you do not know who you are or why you are here, the truth can be used against you by those who pride themselves on manipulative lies, putting the Big O on your mission.

What is the Big O? It is a chokehold or yoke! This holding process is similar to a wedding ring, symbolizing a married person, representing their covenant. On the other hand, the ring of omission does the same; it symbolizes the hold on your mission from the Garden of Eden with Adam and Eve. Unfortunately, it will serve its purpose if you allow it to do so, but you also have the POWER to bring it to a complete halt.

More importantly, the Big O applies to any area of your life and to whomever you are dealing with, including your children. What do our children have to do with this? You will never have to train your children on how to do wrong; it is already within them. However, you must train them to do right, behave, share, and exhibit respect with a disciplinary plan you set forth or in motion.

Teaching your children the DIFFERENCE between the right and wrong ways of doing things gives them a better understanding of how to navigate through good and bad, just and unjust, right and wrong, positive and negative, and so on. Doing so builds character in the teacher-student and student-teacher relations in all walks of life, from personal to professional, and all the way to doing business.

Now, getting back to business...if you consciously decide to remove the chokehold or yoke from your mind, your mission will follow suit, and no one or nothing can hold you back from Divine Achievement, especially when you begin to PLAN according to your Predestined Blueprint, or your reason for being. However, if you do not know this or fall for the okey-doke, you will 'get got' by deceptive measures. Nevertheless, this chapter aims to help you recognize some of the pitfalls associated with the chokehold of the Big O, causing it to stub its toe, instead of you stubbing yours, especially when it comes down to your Divine Mission.

When individuals or businesses fail to plan for success, they often react to situations rather than proactively anticipate them. Unfortunately, this can lead to missed opportunities to capitalize on trends or emerging technologies. Additionally, without a clear plan in place, resources may be wasted on ineffective strategies or initiatives that do not align with the goals of the individual or business.

Furthermore, not planning for success can lead to a lack of direction and purpose. Without clear goals and objectives, individuals and businesses may struggle to stay motivated and focused, leading to a lack of progress and ultimate failure to achieve the desired outcome.

In addition, omission can lead to a lack of accountability and responsibility, hindering innovation and progress. If important ideas or feedback are omitted, it can prevent us from identifying areas for improvement or developing new and innovative strategies designed to help us stay competitive, relevant, and useful.

Overall, it is essential to become mindful of the potential negative impacts of omission, taking steps to ensure all vital information and responsibilities are communicated effectively and addressed promptly. Listed below are a few ways to deal with the *Pitfalls of Omission*, but not limited to such:

- ☐ Research the topic, gathering factual information.
- ☐ Ask questions to clarify the issue, situation, circumstance, or event.
- ☐ Check multiple sources to ensure accuracy.
- ☐ Use fact-checking websites to verify claims.
- ☐ Consult with experts, consultants, or mentors.
- ☐ Look for patterns of bias or misinformation.
- ☐ Consider the source of the information.
- ☐ Share your findings with others.
- ☐ Encourage open and honest communication.
- ☐ Advocate for transparency and accountability.
- ☐ Educate yourself and others about critical thinking.
- ☐ Speak up when you notice omissions or inaccuracies.
- ☐ Challenge false or misleading statements.
- ☐ Use data and evidence to support your arguments.
- ☐ Engage in constructive dialogue.
- ☐ Have the tough conversations.
- ☐ Avoid personal attacks or insults.
- ☐ Stay calm and rational, even in heated discussions.
- ☐ Foster values of truth-seeking and integrity.
- ☐ Hold yourself and others accountable for honesty and accuracy.
- ☐ Always add the Holy Trinity into the equation.

What can this list do for us? It assists in getting rid of the fluff. Planning for success is essential for individuals and businesses to achieve their goals and reach their full potential. Individuals and businesses can increase their chances of success by proactively anticipating challenges and opportunities, focusing resources on effective strategies, and maintaining a clear sense of direction and purpose with the facts.

The *Pitfalls of Omission* are real, whether you are in the know or out of it. Not having a clear understanding of your impact on society and the environment when doing business will cause you to overlook what you should pay attention to, primarily when your mission depends on them.

Doing life, business, and Divine Purpose, *As It Pleases God*, are designed to propel you to the next level of GREATNESS, even if you are clueless about them. For this reason, according to your Predestined Blueprint, you should never allow cluelessness to become an excuse for not learning about the BENEFITS associated with operating at your FULL POTENTIAL.

Chapter Two
The Wise Blueprint

The Wise Blueprint is hidden in our WHY. So, the relevant question is, 'Why do we need Wisdom?' The truth is, 'Wisdom needs us!' Standalone Wisdom does not work without a VESSEL using it. We cannot see it, but it is just as real as the Law of Gravity. Divine Wisdom is drawn to our Spiritual Core; if we do not know this, we will opt for standalone knowledge without Divine Wisdom. In contrast, the goal of *The WHY Blueprint* is to possess both, knowing how to use them, *As It Pleases God*.

Why do we need knowledge and Divine Wisdom, especially if we have it going on with deep pockets, operating wisely? Unfortunately, we will see how far our deep pockets will go when we need what money cannot buy. What does this mean? What will we do when we need to break a yoke from within? What will we do when our family is under Spiritual Attack, and our money cannot fix it for them? Inarguably, this is a question we will ALL face at some point, so it behooves us to prepare, preventively getting in the KNOW about Spiritual Matters.

    Beyond any doubt, if we do not know what money cannot buy, it indicates we are already operating in a soulish deficit. How can I say such a thing, right? I wish the best for everyone; thus, I am also Spiritually Ordained to UNVEIL the truth. Here is what we must know: *"Whoever shuts his ears to the cry of the poor will also cry himself and not be heard. A gift in secret pacifies anger, and a bribe behind the back, strong wrath."* Proverbs 21:13-14. We often think this scripture refers only to life's tangibles. Undoubtedly, it is not speaking solely of outward poverty and crying; it refers to inward pacifiers and silence from within the human psyche, spreading outwardly.

    When speaking of people experiencing poverty, we often think about people with little or no income, but this is not just about money; it is about Mental, Physical, Emotional, and most of all, SPIRITUAL NEGLECT. If we can sleep in peace knowing we can help someone, encourage them, or offer compassionate support without trying to do so, something is wrong. The seeds of hope, love, faith, encouragement, and community have POWER, keeping us upright with our Heavenly Father. If we opt NOT to use our seeds positively or we use them selfishly, our psyche benefits, affecting our people skills unambiguously behind closed doors.

    On the other hand, if we offer help, kindness, or whatever to those in need, and they REJECT it or attempt to USE us for selfish gain, we are free and clear to move on, shaking the dust off our feet. Matthew 10:14 advises: *"And whoever will not receive you nor hear your words, when you depart from that house or city, shake off the dust from your feet."* Sometimes, it may be the hardest thing to do, but we must protect our sanity, exercising Divine Wisdom, *As It Pleases God.*

What is the purpose of shaking the dust off our feet? The enemy will use those we love the most to derail, distract, or thwart our Predestined Blueprint. In this event, we must move forward in the Spirit of Excellence, using the Fruits of the Spirit and behaving Christlike, regardless of what the naysayers say. Why? Without walking a day in our shoes, they will get us soulishly jacked up and traumatized by their opinions, causing us to engage in folly or follow an unwise path to destruction. Then again, they may create a path of disobedience in the Eye of God. With this being said, we must incorporate Him in all things, even when dealing with those we love dearly.

What is the purpose of setting Spiritual Boundaries once possessing Divine Wisdom? Regardless of who we are or why we are here, the human psyche is a bottomless pit, wanting more and more. After the thrill is gone, we will look for another fix of whatever with whomever, leading to some form of insecurity or cover-up. For this reason, we will begin lying to ourselves as if we do not know we are lying.

Then again, we may find ourselves pointing fingers or blaming others for what we are also guilty of, without considering self-correcting or self-mirroring. As Spiritual Beings having a human experience, no one person is better than the next; we will all go through this process. The difference is KNOWING what to do when it happens or how to counteract it with positivity before the seed takes root or becomes a seed-bearing fruit.

How to become WISE with *The WHY Blueprint*? First, we must understand what we all have in common...the MAKER of our Divine Blueprint. Secondly, we must know this: *"A good name is to be chosen rather than great riches, Loving favor rather than silver and gold. The rich and the poor have this in common, The LORD is the maker of them all."* Proverbs 22:1-2. And lastly, "By humility and the fear of the LORD are riches and honor and life." Proverbs 22:4. Is this too hard for us to do? Better yet, what if we choose not to do this? *"Thorns and snares are in the way of the perverse; He who guards his soul will be far from them. Train up a child in the way he should go, and when he is old he will not depart from it."* Proverbs 22:5-6.

Purposeful Intents

What is the purpose of using the Bible in *The Wise Blueprint*? Using the Bible as a projector instead of a corrector, we will find ourselves on the leading edge of destruction without Spiritual Direction. What does this mean? Biblical Wisdom is a Spiritual Tool of correction, grounding, pruning, regrafting, and redirection. Characteristically, it should not be used as a projecting tool or a rod, primarily if correction is not occurring within us. It makes us appear like wolves in sheep's clothing or a hypocrite. Really? Yes, really!

Should we not use the Bible as a weapon of warfare? Of course, we should! Still, we cannot limit it to warfare alone, particularly when misusing or abusing its use to manipulate, connive, bully, or scheme like the enemy. What if we do? Sadly, we become the enemy to ourselves, putting a halt on our Divine Mission with limitations until we consciously decide to work on ourselves, *As It Pleases God*.

Why would we become limited in what we were called to do? The Bible we use in Spiritual Warfare as Believers, or cursing someone as the enemy, also has Spiritual Contingencies we often overlook. Does the enemy really use the Bible in such a manner? From what I have seen with my physical and Spiritual Eyes, the enemy often knows the Bible better than Believers, out-praying and circling hoops around us with all things Spiritual. And this is why they laugh at

Believers...as we call evil good and good evil. Really? Yes, really!

Spiritual Contingencies

My ear has been to the ground for some time now. I have seen Believers, including myself, idolize enemies, not realizing who they are, violating the conscience, downplaying the obvious, or opting not to know to satiate a hidden want, need, desire, or trauma. Inarguably, no one is exempt from this learning curve. Still, we must develop a Spiritual Awareness, enabling us to snap out of our self-induced comas, learn the associated lessons, and use it as ammunition for a win-win in our Testimony to help the next person. While at the same time, Divinely Aligning with the Spiritual Contingencies set forth, gathering the relevant and sustainable information to feed God's sheep and unveil our Predestined Blueprint.

What are the Spiritual Contingencies? There are many, but the ones for *The WHY Blueprint* are the Fruits of the Spirit, putting on the Whole Armor of God, and Spiritually Tilling our own ground, determining the worldly from the Kingdomly. What does this mean? Our fruits determine whether we are using the Bible correctly or incorrectly. Simply put, *"You will know them by their fruits."* Matthew 7:16.

In addition, it will also determine the durability of our Spiritual Armor, which we will discuss in another chapter. Regardless of the fruits we bear right now, we must use the Bible as a Spiritual Mirror of self-analysis, self-correction, or self-reflection. Suppose we use the Word of God without the ability to repent, give thanks, exhibit compassion, or extend mercy. In this case, we will inadvertently rebuke ourselves, putting a damper on *The WHY Blueprint* because we are not behaving sensibly in the precursor stages of *The Wise Blueprint*. Are they not the same? No, they are not; we cannot move to *The WHY Blueprint* with foolery. Once again, we will get rebuked.

How is it possible to rebuke ourselves? Our self-talk, thoughts, behaviors, biases, and emotions will determine our level of self-reproof. When our motives are not up to par, *As It Pleases God*, it becomes difficult to understand the difference between positive and negative, right and wrong, just and unjust, and so on. Blasphemy, right? Wrong! Our Spiritual Fruits of Love, Joy, Peace, Patience, Kindness, Goodness, Faithfulness, Gentleness, and Self-Control speak for themselves, providing liberation, protection, unyoking, and understanding.

Allow Wisdom to Speak

Unbeknown to most, our Predestined Blueprint has a VOICE, speaking to us even when we ignore it, doing what we want to do. Then again, if we do not know what we were called to do, we just do not know, right? Well, let *The Wise Blueprint* have the floor for a moment; it will speak for itself:

- ☐ *The Wise Blueprint* says, 'You must humbly know you are WISE.' It is not easy to evolve into what you do not believe. If you think you are unwise, you will make unwise decisions. On the other hand, if you think you are smart, you will begin making intelligent decisions. Our decisions tell us what we believe about ourselves without saying one word. Although we are all subjected to error, our correction efforts say much more than leaving negative behaviors, thoughts, beliefs, or whatever as-is.

- *The Wise Blueprint* says, 'Your past was designed to PREPARE you with knowledge, experience, understanding, and know-how.' Your faith and hope in the NOW bridge the gap from your past to your future, positively or negatively. So, keep it positive, productive, and fruitful.

- *The Wise Blueprint* says, 'You must be willing to maximize every moment given, while being grateful for everything, regardless of how it appears to the naked eye.' Why must we become grateful? Ungratefulness and doubt minimize our now, instead of maximizing what we have in our hands. Remember, we already possess the Spiritual Tools to make our names GREAT; we only need to learn how to use them, *As They Please God.*

- *The Wise Blueprint* says, 'You must become patient in your thoughts, actions, beliefs, and words.' If not, impatience will become our greatest downfall, causing us to miss out or overlook what is in plain sight.

- *The Wise Blueprint* says, 'You must be prepared with a plan of action, and remain proactively on ready.' Unpreparedness causes most people to miss out on what is Divine. For example, we will never see a professional athlete avoid preparing unless their goal is to lose. Nevertheless, with *The WHY Blueprint*, we prepare to WIN by becoming WISE first!

- *The Wise Blueprint* says, 'You must focus on what you are doing, getting rid of unjustified distractions.' I do not need to define a distraction; you know what distracts you from doing what needs to be done.

- *The Wise Blueprint* says, 'Remember that the low-hanging fruits are just as important as the high ones.' Therefore, put everything and everyone into their proper perspective.

- *The Wise Blueprint* says, 'Get in position.' There is no reason to walk around with your head hanging down. When it is time to swing, you must already be in position. The Pitcher will not wait for you; He will strike you out of the game, moving to the next in line. Everything is preparing you; you must pay attention to what is happening around you and within you.

- *The Wise Blueprint* says, 'What makes you weak is the same thing that makes you strong! It is all in your MINDSET.' Transfer negativity into positivity; they both take the same amount of effort. If you look for the good in all things, you will find it. Once you do, extract the lesson, learn from it, pinpoint the win-win, and share it with someone else. Does it work? I am living proof. I learn from everything, good, bad, or indifferent. Then, I convert it into Divine Wisdom for the next man. When activating the Law of Reciprocity as such, the Divine Well of Wisdom continues to overflow, getting everyone crossing my path drenched.

- *The Wise Blueprint* says, 'Judge no one, use the Fruits of the Spirit, and behave Christlike, and things money cannot buy will find you.' What if we just want money, and that is it? Unfortunately, if this is all they want, I automatically know they are operating with mangled fruits, judgmentally biased, and keeled character. How is it possible to know this? When operating with the lust of the eyes, lusts of the flesh, and the pride of life, it indicates underlying jealousy, envy, pride, greed, coveting, competitiveness, and pompousness.

  Is this not judging the book by its cover? Absolutely not! I am only judging the FRUITS by its cover. According to the Bible, there is no Spiritual Law against judging, understanding, or reading fruits. More importantly, I will use the Fruits of the Spirit to treat you properly with love, kindness, respect, and gentleness regardless. It is just designed to let me know WHAT and WHO I am dealing with to protect my Spiritual Crown, Fruits, and Anointing.

What is the purpose of knowing what *The Wise Blueprint* says? When attempting to be in Purpose on purpose, we must take into account a few things:

- The QUALITY of our message.
- The QUALITY of our delivery.
- The QUALITY of our content.
- The QUALITY of our speaking abilities.

What if we do not have any of them? It is okay...this is WHY I am here. Our Divine Purpose will always contain a message. If we do not know what it is, we cannot determine what it is NOT. In short, a *Spirit to Spirit* Connection must be made with our Heavenly Father and documented accordingly.

According to the Heavenly of Heavens, God likes things decent and in order. What does this mean? We must PREPARE. According to our Predestined Blueprint, the content, resources, or direction we need will flow once we prepare, *As It Pleases Him*. If it does not flow, we must check our cistern; it may be the wrong one, we are operating in the flesh, we are serving rotten fruits, or our character sucks.

Notably, when the Holy Spirit uses us to convey a message according to our Predestined Blueprint, it has a certain tone, inflection, or swag, regardless of whether we are good at speaking or not. Fortunately, this is how I can tell the shakers from the bakers and the wannabes from the soon-to-be. Is this not judging? Absolutely not! I have worked to develop my Spiritual Eyes, Ears, and Voice to know the difference. And so can you! This discerning process is similar to knowing the sound of rain, thundering, wind, or your child's voice. So, do not be deceived; *Spirit knows Spirit*.

The loudest voice we will ever hear is the one inside of us. In fact, we must learn and master what our inner voice is saying to and about us, others, and the Holy Trinity. In addition, we must do it without allowing the negative chatter to drown out our capacity to hear clearly from the inside out. Now, if someone or something is drowning out our inner voice with negativity, abuse, disrespect, or yelling, this should serve as a RED FLAG that trauma to the psyche is on the way. This internal flaw is one of the reasons why the Bible says, *"Better to dwell in a corner of a housetop, than in a house shared with a contentious woman."* Proverbs 21:9.

What about the Voice of God? Is it not loud? Most often, the Voice of God is a still small voice. If we ever hear Him speak loudly, it will literally shake us to the core. Usually, the LOUDNESS will ONLY happen during impending danger or when He gives specific instructions to flee immediately.

The Spiritual Light we carry from within starts with knowing our Spiritual Passion, Creativity, and Purpose. As Believers, this is not the typical passion, creativity, or purpose we use daily; we must dig deep to unveil our reason for being. Why must we dig deep? Our Predestined Blueprint is hidden within them, similar to a diamond in the rough.

Once we begin recognizing or working on our Divine Blueprint, our Spiritual Tools, Teacher, Understanding, and Wisdom must come forth. What if they are not forthcoming? Then, we need to check the BLUEPRINT to determine whether it is self-created or Godly Ordained.

We often seek tools, understanding, skills, and wisdom without knowing what we are born to do, plugging and playing, or making up stuff off the cuff. As a result, we meander through life using mixed-matched tools, borrowed understanding, and worldly knowledge, having nothing to do with our Blueprinted Purpose. As a result, we get lost in the shuffle, losing our way HOME because we cannot reach our goals, or if we do, we are UNSATISFIED.

Chapter Three
H.O.M.E. Base

Are you feeling lost, hopeless, or detached from reality? Are you aimlessly wandering through life, looking for the next quick fix? Are you experiencing any feelings of confusion or disorientation? Are you struggling to focus or concentrate on the people, places, and things needing your attention? Although relevant protoplasmic questions need answers, our genetic homing system also requires attention.

Why would our homing system need us, especially when we do not know what it is? Regardless of whether we are clueless about our H.O.M.E. Base or homing system, we can feel it within the human psyche. We may not consciously know its technical name, but the feeling from within each of us knows, and the longing does not go away. We can cover it up with something or someone else as a temporary fix, but the truth is, the SIGNAL does not relent. Why? We are Spiritual Beings having a human experience, even if we are clueless about SPIRITUALITY.

According to the Ancient of Days, it is time to use the PREWIRED Spiritual Tools at our fingertips. While at the same time, using the information readily available at our beck and call, without blaming the Devil! What does this mean? We will find ourselves laying the blame without taking accountability for knowing who we are, why we are, and how we are. Candidly, my questions in this matter are:

- ☐ Do you know what or who you are?
- ☐ Do you know what and who you are not?
- ☐ Are you aware of your Spiritual Tools?
- ☐ Do you even care to know?
- ☐ Are you blaming the Devil for your aloofness?
- ☐ Are you willing to become an authentic work-in-progress?

What if we get lost or confused when becoming a work-in-progress, *As It Pleases God*? It is natural to stumble, get confused, or get lost occasionally. Without getting lost, we may NOT find a new direction, path, skill, lesson, seed, or way of doing things. Why? According to the Heavenly of Heavens, the challenge is GENIUS!

Those who do not CHALLENGE themselves to become better, stronger, and wiser, *As It Pleases God*, cannot tap into their Genius Capabilities, Divine Blueprint, or H.O.M.E. Base. They will only have access to counterfeit versions or limited gifts with negative characteristics of jealousy, envy, pride, greed, anger, hatred, nastiness, and coveting attached.

Do we not all have equal rights to Divine Access? Absolutely! *"God is no respecter of persons."* Acts 10:34. We are all equal and deserving of love and respect, regardless of social status, race, gender, or other characteristics. Yet, seeing our Divine Access from a distance is not ideal for our Heaven on Earth Experience.

Why must we view our Divine Access from a distance? When we become worse, weaker, and more foolish, playing God without consciously attempting to self-correct, He views us like the Tower of Babel, changing our Spiritual Language. Then again, He may see us as Moses, viewing the Promised Land from afar. Once this happens, disobedience, rebellion, unrepentance, pompousness, and unbridled weaknesses pump the brakes on our Spiritual Encounters, even if we are Believers who are Holy Ghost-Filled and Fire-Baptized.

When it is all said and done, according to *The WHY Blueprint*, we must learn how to recalibrate ourselves back to H.O.M.E. Base without shifting responsibility or playing the blame game. Simply put, our seeds will always look for a home with or without our permission. In the same way, God does not discriminate against us; our seeds DO NOT discriminate. Whatever we set in motion, positively or negatively, will come home to roost. Without further ado, here is what the H.O.M.E. means: Humbleness of Mind and Emotions.

HUMBLENESS
OF
MIND
EMOTIONS

According to the Heavenly of Heavens, we cannot truly find our way HOME if we cannot exhibit the Humbleness of Mind and Emotions. Whenever we feel lost, confused, misled, abandoned, or whatever, we must check our

HOMING SYSTEM connected to our H.O.M.E. Base. What is the difference? The ultimate difference is in the CONNECTION. For example, if we have a security system, the cameras and base communicate, recording footage based on the established settings. The same applies to us. When we are humble, especially in our thoughts, emotions, and behaviors, it keeps our Spiritual Compass calibrated and working properly, according to our Predestined Blueprint.

On the other hand, when we lack humility or become irrationally emotional, we create static in our Divine Connection. Unfortunately, unchecked or ungoverned breakdowns within the human psyche cause skips and breaks in our footage...Spiritual Footage, to be exact. What does this mean? We tend to forget or not remember the occurring or recurring lapses in our charactorial behaviors or thoughts. Moreover, we break the Divine Connection of our *Spirit to Spirit* Relations with the Holy Trinity without buffering and reconnecting.

Undoubtedly, we all have our moments...still, we are designed to self-correct, self-repent, self-mirror, self-buffer, and reconnect to our H.O.M.E. Base automatically. If this does not happen with the conscience, we must check our Spiritual Connection.

What is the big deal, especially when we all have emotions? Of course, we all have emotions, but when our emotions have us, we have a problem. Why would we have a problem, particularly when we are entitled to feel how we want? First, when our emotions get the best of us, we will set false expectations of God, ourselves, and others, leading to our disappointments, frustrations, and compounded issues. Secondly, we will battle with an ungoverned tongue, negative mental chatter, and internally destructive habits.

According to the Heavenly of Heavens, we are equipped with PREWIRED TOOLS (Building Blocks) to zero in on our reason for being. However, we must pay close attention to our SEEDLINGS or SEEDERY (Character Traits). Why? Life forces us to till our own ground. Hence, we must know how to plant, extract, regraft, and reverse engineer to benefit the Kingdom, ourselves, and others.

For our sake, God deals with our INTENTS to determine our readiness, Spiritual Classroom, whether we must return to the cycle of déjà vu, if our fruits are palatable, or where pruning must occur. For this reason, *The WHY Blueprint* is loaded with Seeds of Hope, Love, Faith, and Oneness. If we Spiritually Till, *As It Pleases God*, WHAT and WHO we need will find us.

How do we extract the Seeds of Hope, Love, Faith, and Oneness? Once again, we need Spiritual Tools. Outside of our charactorial tools, we are going to deal with three Toolable Handles or Coverings first:

- ☐ The Handle of Surrender (Surrendering to the Cause).
- ☐ The Handle of Submission (Submit to the Assignment).
- ☐ The Handle of Sharing (Agree to Share).

Unbeknown to most, we are a giant plant, tree, vine, seed, and root possessing fruits. How is this possible? We are all connected, serving a unique purpose. What does this mean? We contain internal steps, systems, strategies, niches, and time capsules, aligning with our reason for being and Divine Responsibilities. Unfortunately, they are all covered by our something else, issues, weaknesses, setbacks, biases, and so on. For this reason, we all need *The WHY Blueprint* to unveil our true capacity for GREATNESS.

What makes *The WHY Blueprint* so unique? We provide the Know-How and the How-To with a Divine Understanding,

As It Pleases God. In addition, we offer a check and balance system or checklists to help self-correct amid differences, misunderstandings, stumbling blocks, or internal qualms, helping one to dig deep.

My Seed, My Root, and My Fruit

Please allow me to share the WHY behind the writer in me. I struggled with writing at a young age due to cultural differences, biased divides, and a non-writing environment. Words never seemed to flow from my mind to the page as quickly as they did for others. I had to filter what was in my mind from what was coming out of my mouth. In addition, being from the country (a little small town), I was not as articulate and outspoken as the city folks. It was not that I had nothing to say; trust me, I had a lot to say.

In my culture, a child had to remain in a child's place with respect, bridling their tongue. By remaining in this little cocoon, I could not express myself in an impactful and engaging way. Nor could I voice my thoughts or opinions without offending, talking too much, exposing truths, or telling people's hidden secrets.

From back then until now, I am a country girl who picked oranges after school and on the weekends, who truly understands the Power of Fruits and Seasons. Although others had the luxury of eating fruits without laboring, I was grafted into a childhood of working to earn my keep. What does this mean in layman's terms? If I wanted to eat, have a roof over my head, clothes on my back, and a bed to sleep in, I had to work for it.

While I picked oranges, I was hoping and praying for a better future while simultaneously struggling with a Gift of Prophecy and Spiritual Discernment. As a child, this was a lot to handle. Why? I could not understand the big issue of writing in my native tongue, speaking what came to mind, holding my tongue, and working to care for myself as a child, especially after losing my Grandmother. She was the only one who taught me how to balance my Spiritual Gifts with reality.

Unfortunately, I was on my own after the loss. Still, I knew I was different and felt God chose this life for me. By no means would I settle for defeat, especially when I was answering adult questions and solving adult problems in a child's body.

As a student, I dreaded writing assignments because my home language did not match the English Language I was taught. My mom said it was right, and my teacher said it was wrong. I was oblivious to what was right and wrong or who was right or wrong as I was caught up in this back-and-forth cycle. Although I was an obedient and intelligent child, this was a bit much. How so? Each time I was prompted to write, I would freeze up, struggling to form a coherent and complete sentence, not knowing whose expectations to follow.

Why would the freeze-ups happen, especially when in school to learn? First, I was confused between slang and good grammar. Secondly, I suffered my first brain injury from a direct hit by a semi-tractor-trailer at a young age. Frankly, this accident happened after recovering from being hit in the eye with a bat by a kid several years prior. Amid the double whammy, I had to still work through my injuries, blacking out from time to time, and still having to earn my keep, regardless of the pain.

As my Grandmother was no longer my crutch, I had to learn how to TRUST and LEAN on God Almighty. Was it difficult? Absolutely! I was a child. However, I knew education was my way out...For this reason, clarity was key, and understanding the WHY was the gateway. Although my grades did not suffer, my confidence did. Why? I was silenced...I had to become SILENT to the confusion, to earning my keep, and to my bodily afflictions.

All in all, I was pounced upon at home for speaking good grammar and correcting bad grammar. It was a triple-whammy at school because I was slicing and dicing good grammar while getting the laughs and smirks for being countrified. This situation led to being bullied for using the wrong words or incorrect grammar without knowing it was incorrect.

When there are cultural differences in the classroom, children secretly give up on themselves. Why do they give up easily? They are caught between what is correct and what is not. For me, it can no longer be ignored!

I felt like my inability to write was holding me back from achieving my goals due to the challenges of speaking English in two different ways. But I refused to give up. I knew writing was a skill that could be improved with practice and dedication. Therefore, I started reading and journaling more, immersing myself in different writing styles, and learning from the masters to develop my own, even with my mistakes and issues.

In any event, I began documenting the Divine Instructions given to me in my *Spirit to Spirit* Communion, laying a roadmap of where I started and my Blueprinted Destination. Slowly but surely, I began to see progress, becoming better, stronger, and wiser, *As It Pleased God*. With the will to survive against all odds, regardless of how my life appeared to the naked eye or what I did or did not have, I refused to allow anyone or anything to invoke doubt, fear, or insecurities in my life, my writing abilities, or my Predestined Blueprint.

As my writings became more polished, I received positive feedback, with a few sidebar jokes about my previous or current inadequacies, as if it were a laughing matter. Despite the prolonged mockery, I considered it a part of my LEARNING JOURNEY, placing a Spiritual Seal on The WHY Blueprint. Here is the kicker: the ones who were laughing with the sidebar jokes were asking me how to spell words, using words out of context, not pronouncing everyday words correctly, or asking me to write for them.

Sadly, they were projecting how they felt about themselves on me. They had real nerves to insult me or my WHY, but I still had to remain kind, respectful, forgiving, and helpful, using the Fruits of the Spirit and choosing to take the STORY instead. It is not that I do not make mistakes occasionally; I do have enough sense to use spell check before dragging someone through the dirt, laughing at them, or ruining their credibility.

What is the big deal about mistakes or being error-free? First, no perfect writer exists; even if we pretend that we are, we occasionally make errors. Fortunately, this is why editors are in business. Secondly, we cannot judge someone for doing something we do not dare to do ourselves. Thirdly, we are all a work-in-progress!

The deal is that I am writing, using my Gifts, Calling, Talents, and Creativity to encourage and motivate for the GREATER GOOD, offering a helping hand regardless of my differences or idiosyncrasies. I am not here to discourage, criticize, or laugh at others doing their best with what they have. Nor am I here to knock the next person trying to become better, stronger, and wiser.

Bottom line, I am here to do my part in the Spirit of Excellence, and if someone has a problem with it, then it is their problem, not mine. If they could walk in my shoes, God would have given them the Spiritual Blueprint to UNVEIL the veiled for a time such as this. As I continued my Spiritual Journey with a Positive Mindset, I realized how my words could impact those with a willing ear to hear, as my Gift began to make room for me.

With much Divine Training, many Spiritual Classrooms, and the Rod of Correction, I mastered knowing when to speak and hold my tongue. While simultaneously articulating the Divine Message from the Heavenly of Heavens into a palatable language for the hearer. What does this mean? With excellent people skills, *As It Pleases God*, I can speak the language of those from the small towns to the big cities and anything in between, leaving no man behind.

If I am misunderstood or underestimated, my heart posture, fruits, and character will speak louder than any articulated words, thoughts, or beliefs. How is this possible? The Fruits of the Spirit and Christlike Character do not need a voice; they only need willingness, humility, and opportunity.

As I documented my issues, solutions, goals, plans, and unique journey, using the Fruits of the Spirit and Christlike Character, they INSPIRED and MOTIVATED me to take action. How? I began moving, thinking, and believing, *As It Pleased God*, not myself. Activating the Law of Reciprocity and connecting with others on a deeper level by using Spiritual Principles changed my life's trajectory. I may not have started with an obvious talent or seed. Still, with hard work and determination, Spiritually Tilling my own ground, my seeds became rooted and grounded, budding into a tree bearing much fruit.

I am proud to say I am a confident and skilled writer, sharing *The WHY Blueprint* with others as the Tree of Life. Besides, I throw in a little slang every now and then, just because I CAN, with no shame attached!

What would a child do when caught between slang and good grammar? They must read books and learn without settling for defeat. If we do not read, our intellectual capacity gets lost in the shuffle through the issues of life, making us susceptible to mockery. Unbeknown to most, the confusion is real, and for some, they give up due to the bullying associated with the great divide of speaking correct English. However, the most relevant solution is to READ books. Can this really help us? Yes, especially when we read aloud; this keeps our natural tongue from superseding the correct dialect.

Simply put, every child should be reading aloud instead of to themselves, especially when slang is involved. Doing so helps them to pronounce and spell words correctly. For example, I was brought up saying the word 'nutneg,' when it should have been 'nutmeg.' I did not learn the difference until I was a full-grown adult, going to the store looking for 'nutneg,' and could not find it on the shelf. I asked the clerk for help, and they asked, 'Are you referring to nutmeg?' Then I realized I was pronouncing it wrong until that very moment. Unfortunately, we did not have Google back then; we had the good old dictionary.

In what situations is it appropriate to use slang in professional settings? When using slang in professional settings, it is important to consider the context and audience. Generally, it is best to avoid using slang in professional communication, as it can be perceived as unprofessional or disrespectful. It is always essential to use good judgment and err on the side of caution when deciding whether or not to use slang in a professional setting.

There are several ways to enhance language skills, such as reading books and articles, listening to podcasts or audiobooks, watching movies or TV shows with subtitles, and practicing writing and speaking with native speakers or language tutors. It may take time and effort, but anyone can improve their grammar and language skills with persistence and dedication.

Many struggle to balance using slang with proper grammar in everyday conversations; they just do not mention it. Using slang in different social settings can have both benefits and drawbacks. When speaking with friends or family casually, slang may be appropriate, helping to create a more relaxed and friendly atmosphere, and it can also help to build rapport with others. However, using too much slang or using it in inappropriate contexts can be seen as unprofessional or disrespectful. In more formal or professional settings, sticking to proper grammar and avoiding slang can help to convey a more polished and competent image.

How can we solve this issue? Once again, READ OUT LOUD, pronouncing every word correctly! If it worked for me, it would work for you, regardless of where you are from and who raised you. I was not born with a silver spoon in my mouth. I was raised picking oranges and became creative using junk with zero dollars involved; therefore, no one can say I do not know what I am speaking about. I know all too well, and DO NOT settle for excuses for not trying, giving up on yourself, or not sharing your story as a TESTAMENT for the next man. So, in *The WHY Blueprint*, my question is, 'What is Your Story?'

CHAPTER FOUR
The WHY Blueprint

The WHY Blueprint is designed for the *As It Pleases God®* Movement, bringing us in Purpose on purpose, using the Spiritual Tools, Principles, and Experiences that are at our fingertips. Of course, we are all entitled to do what we desire; however, when it comes to our Predestined Blueprint, which contains its own set of Divine Provisions, Treasures, Wisdom, and Secrets, we are not of our own. We belong to our Heavenly Father, and He will not open His Mighty Hands without us using what we already have in ours.

The WHY Blueprint incorporates the intermingling of deep seeds, roots, and fruits, maximizing their extraction and conversion to bring our stability and passion to the forefront with no shame attached. What if we omit this process? By omitting this process, we subject ourselves to the hit-and-miss, bait-and-switch, trial-and-error, or crash-and-burn mentality instead of becoming a bona fide work-in-progress. According to the Heavenly of Heavens, we choose our hard or soft when missing the connecting or bonding factors hidden within our seeds, roots, and fruits. For example, when playing baseball, we can have a correct stance, be the fastest runner on the team, and have hyped-up confidence from the crowd's cheers. Still, if we cannot CONNECT the bat to the ball, we will strike ourselves out of the game, regardless of how much we trained for that moment. The same applies to our Predestined Blueprint; we must Divinely Connect to the Originator and then TRAIN for the game.

To get to the ROOT of the matter of anything or with anyone, we must account for the SEEDS and analyze the FRUITS, *As It Pleases God*. Why is it so crucial in *The WHY Blueprinting* process? It is two-fold: What Hurts You is What Heals You.

What Hurts You *is* **What Heals You**

How can what hurts us possibly heal us? According to the Heavenly of Heavens, this is how Divine Training occurs, even in nature. For example, a snake bite is cured with antivenom. Although there are many variations of cures, the healing or neutralizing components of a snake's venom are hidden within itself through a complex mixture of enzymes, proteins, and other molecules. Then again, it can be crossed-gened or gene-mapped with another venomous animal. More importantly, if one does not know what they are doing, they can cause more harm than good. The same applies to us with this analogy. What we need is ALREADY within us in a strategic or compounded composition. If we do not know what we are doing and why, we will turn on ourselves!

Suppose we do not allow what hurts us to heal us. Opting not to heal creates improper healing with a reopening scab. Band-Aids and scabs are not what God has in mind for us. Why? Our wounds will continuously reopen with associated triggers, threats, or thoughts, causing us to ooze everywhere, getting on those we encounter. The goal is to have fully healed scars, reminding us of the journey or encouraging us to move forward positively in the Spirit of Excellence with established preventative measures in place.

Whether you are scabbed, scarred, or using bandages, it is challenging to pinpoint seeds, roots, or fruits when stuck on negative thinking or wallowing in the victim mentality. Why? It is due to the 'woe unto me' mentality, the lies you tell yourself, constant denial, and underlying selfishness. Although everyone hurts and heals differently, no one can do this for you; you must want to heal for yourself.

The WHY Blueprint helps us to think introspectively and wisely, even if we do not like being questioned. According to the Ancient of Days, personal question-and-answer sessions are required to become GREAT. Based upon our DNA, to get to the real root of any problem, we must journey through the WHY; if not, we will only deal with surface issues or symptoms with surface results.

Our WHY in life or the WHY from within can be multi-leveled, multi-surfaced, or multi-generational, even if we have it going on. Thus, we must document them, their offspring, and distant relatives, leaving no stone unturned. Why should we dig deep? It removes assumptions, lies, and deceitful debauchery. We can only go so far with lies, whereas the truth continuously gives us what we need as long as we remain open, teachable, humble, and astute.

For example, I was online using a new addition to a current system; after they learned from my method of operation, gleaning wisdom, and fixing their glitches to update their system for the betterment, someone vicariously blocked me from accessing relevant information. Learning from someone's maximization and giving them the boot is not a good business practice, especially when doing it undercover, as if I did not know. Unfortunately, taking the easy way out of doing what I do while having a paid membership caused me to give a serious side-eye to their intents, system, and method of operation.

Why would I give a side-eye to an online company? They could have emailed me stating their intent to block me, explained my point of error, or thanked me for the information they gleaned; besides, I am a paying customer. Nevertheless, instead of complaining or placing a dent in my efforts, I go to the WHYs of Divine Wisdom to create my OWN SYSTEM, using them as an example of unblocking the process without regressing. This experience was a prime example of, *'What Hurts You is What Heals You.'* If they had not tried to sucker-punch me with an unfavorable seed, we would not be discussing the favorable rooting system of the fruit right now, and *The WHY Blueprint* would not have been written, bringing the Tree of Life to another. More importantly, when we are in Purpose on purpose, this is how the enemy will become the footstool of our NEXT!

Everything and everyone has a lesson attached. We only need to master the ability to extract and convert a negative into a positive, bad into good, unproductive into productive, wrong into right, and so on, creating a win-win regardless of how it appears.

Why should we master the extraction and conversion process? First, extracting and converting is a MINDSET. Secondly, it develops our recognition skills. Thirdly, it helps us to think on our feet, seeing through people, places, and things with laser vision like Superman. Lastly, it helps us to recognize what we need and respectfully discard what we do not. Our teachable moments come into our lives to help us, not to hurt us. Actually, it is designed to help us think, behave, discern, and choose correctly, tapping into our Well of Divine Wisdom.

Although the Well of Divine Wisdom takes more energy, the key is I know HOW to do it, getting the vital information needed to feed God's sheep. More importantly, by understanding *The WHY Blueprint*, we can create our own and bridge it with another system already in place to assist.

If we tap into a Divine System, *As It Pleases God*, before using man-made ones, we can Divinely Access more information. Why would we have more access? It has a BLUEPRINT attached. With this mindset, the questions will yield, leading us to it, them, or that.

If the informational system leads us away from our Predestined Blueprint, it will NOT yield as it should, causing us to become Mentally, Physically, Emotionally, or Spiritually blocked. What does this mean? We will begin fighting against ourselves, violating our conscience, or becoming confused.

The divide in our conscience is similar to the freshwater and saltwater divisions. What does this analogy mean? A visible line is dividing the two, similar to how the psyche is divided from the conscience invisibly. Once we tap into the Divine System, we can access this invisible line of demarcation. What is the reason for the invisibility? Everything we need is written on the tablet of the heart, aligning our purpose, creativity, talents, and ingenuity; thus, if one does not Spiritually Till their own ground, they become limited to their understanding and not God's Divine Wisdom.

What if we are straddling the fence in this area, not knowing what's what? In this case, our conscience will brackishly mix us (a colorized difference), letting us know something is not right, we are in uncharted territory, we are crossing our boundaries, or we are not ready for whatever, with whomever. This analogy of the conscience is similar to having our vision blurred as our eyes attempt to refocus and align automatically.

Even if our psyche does not alert us...the conscience will; therefore, we must ensure we are listening, learning, and nurturing it. Why? It is designed to serve us like a Spiritual Compass, even when the Holy Spirit lies dormant due to our folly or disobedience. Remember, God will always give us something to work with, and it is our responsibility to find it, use it, and share the results.

Once we understand *The WHY Blueprint* of our reason for being, no one or nothing can hold us back from Divine Greatness, unless we allow them or refuse to put in the work. All else will create a stepping stone, training us for the next step, platform, or transition.

What is so special about *The WHY Blueprint*? You! God has targeted you specifically. With *The WHY Blueprint*, He will UNVEIL the information, instructions, and details unique to you and Him. Just follow my lead, answer the questions, and use your Spiritual Journal to document; He will begin to nudge you like no other.

The WHY Blueprint will mean something totally different for the next person. Why? Their Predestined Blueprint has unique instructions, aligning with only them. Simply put, *The WHY Blueprint* is NOT a one-and-done system; it feeds God's sheep where they are, where they are going, and shows them how to get there, using their own Spiritual Blueprint.

For example, even if someone tries to emulate *The WHY Blueprint's System* or adapt it as the originator, it will NOT be the same. Why? It has my GENETIC CODE attached. I Spiritually Tilled the ground, planted seeds, regrafted roots, nurtured fruits, and pruned branches, *As It Pleased God*. Thus, my Tree of Life is attached to my Bloodline with a multiplicity factor, bringing life to another.

From the Ancient of Days until now, there is no other system on the face of this earth like *The WHY Blueprint*. Our revolving system is designed to target the ROOT and SEED, Mentally, Physically, Emotionally, and Spiritually, teaching how to develop a *Spirit to Spirit* Relationship to download information from the Heavenly of Heavens. Is this not a little arrogant? Absolutely not! In the same way that we all have different fingerprints, footprints, and eyeprints, our Predestined Blueprint does as well. By not knowing this one factor, this is how we 'get got' with the oldest playbook known to man: DECEPTION.

According to our Divinely Blueprinted Code, it is designed to bring us into Purpose on purpose, unveiling what is already within. If one thinks they can do this without God Almighty, then have at it. Once the psyche has its way of running the show, turning you upside down, and deafening you with negativity, causing you to become blind as a bat to your Spirit Man, please let me know how it works out for you on the cycle of déjà vu. What does this have to do with anything? The psyche will run the show, doing a number on you, especially if it is not Spiritually Tamed and Questioned, or when you omit the CREATOR of it all.

Self-Questions
In the same way we have conversations with God, we must also have conversations with ourselves, including the hard

ones. Why? Unfortunately, we become reckless in our actions, thoughts, beliefs, biases, and words by omitting the querying conversational efforts. How do we question or converse with ourselves? It will vary; however, listed below are a few self-questionable conversation starters, but not limited to such:

The Mental WHY Conversational Self-Questions:

1. Why do I need an understanding of ....?
2. Why do I need to achieve ....?
3. Why do I view this as a challenge?
4. Why do I foresee ....?
5. Why do I need to repent about ....?
6. Why do I view this as a risk or roadblock?
7. Why do I need to communicate about ....?
8. Why is maintaining a positive mindset important for my overall well-being?
9. Why do negative thoughts tend to impact me more than positive ones?
10. Why is it important to identify and challenge negative self-talk?
11. Why do I find it difficult to maintain a positive mindset?
12. Why is it vital to surround myself with positive people and influences?
13. Why does focusing on gratitude help me maintain a positive mindset?
14. Why is it imperative to set realistic goals for myself?
15. Why is it essential to practice self-compassion and self-love?
16. Why is it important to forgive myself and others?
17. Why is it beneficial to learn from my mistakes instead of dwelling on them?

18. Why does focusing on solutions instead of problems help me maintain a positive mindset?
19. Why is it important to avoid comparing myself to others?
20. Why is it essential to cultivate a growth mindset?

The Physical WHY Conversational Self-Questions:

1. Why do I prefer ....?
2. Why do I need to shift to ....?
3. Why do I keep doing ....?
4. Why do I avoid ....?
5. Why am I getting red flags about ....?
6. Why does taking care of my physical health impact my level of positivity?
7. Why does engaging in enjoyable activities help me maintain a positive mindset?
8. Why does helping others promote positive feelings within me?
9. Why do mindfulness and meditation help me promote a sustainable connection to myself and God?
10. Why is it important to take breaks and practice self-care?
11. Why do small positive changes add up to big ones?

The Emotional WHY Conversational Self-Questions:

1. Why is it important to control my emotions about ....?
2. Why do I struggle with reacting to ....?
3. Why am I triggered by ....?
4. Why am I provoked by ....?

5. Why do I need to practice self-care when becoming emotional?
6. Why is it difficult to regulate my emotions?
7. Why are episodes of my traumas resurfacing?
8. Why is it important to practice mindfulness?
9. Why do I struggle with hidden bouts of anger, anxiety, stress, or depression?
10. Why is it vital to communicate openly?
11. Why is it essential for me to set boundaries?
12. Why is it imperative to prioritize my emotions?

The Spiritual WHY Conversational Self-Questions:

1. Why do I need faith in ......?
2. Why do I need hope about .....?
3. Why am I ungrateful for ....?
4. Why do I need the Fruits of the Spirit in ......?
5. Why do I need the Holy Trinity involved with ....?
6. Why must I focus on tilling my own ground regarding .....?
7. Why is it important to practice gratitude?
8. Why is it essential to give thanks in all things?
9. Why do I need to put on the Whole Armor of God about ....?
10. Why is my Spirit Man uncomfortable about ....?
11. Why is God speaking to me about ....?
12. Why do I need to respond to God?

The WHY Success Conversational Self-Questions:

1. Why do I consider myself successful?
2. Why do I need to measure my success?

3. Why am I falling short or lacking ....?
4. Why do I think success is essential?
5. Why do I believe that success is attainable?
6. Why do I strive for success?
7. Why do I think success is linked to my Divine Destiny?
8. Why do I think my quality of life is essential to my success?
9. Why do I think positive achievement can impact my passion?
10. Why do I think victory can impact my creativity?
11. Why do I think attainment can impact my confidence?
12. Why do I think achievement can impact my overall well-being?

Why are self-questions important? Simply put, who can question you better than you? Self-questions, self-answers, and self-analysis provide a Spiritual Mirror. If you DOCUMENT your self-queries, you can better navigate other analyses, methodologies, and systems using *The Why Blueprint* system. Therefore, to keep you in the know, I will prepare you to use what you have in your hands, ensuring you can plug and play, take what you need, and grow GREAT, building character, *As It Pleases God*.

Building Character

How we think, feel, and act in different situations matters to our Heavenly Father. Why would it matter, especially when we have free will? It develops our character, habits, attitudes, fruits, seeds, and values that determine the VOLUME of our conscience or Spiritual Compass.

According to the Heavenly of Heavens, we are all born with a soul with our Spiritual Consciousness intact, having a clean slated character plate. After birth, as we build or form our character, our Spiritual Consciousness lays dormant until we consciously choose to be AWAKENED by the Holy Spirit. What does this mean? Our character is NOT something we are born with but is DEVELOPED through our choices, thoughts, conditioning, traumas, actions, biases, or the lack thereof, affecting our relationships with God, ourselves, others, our success, and our Divine Destiny. In this developmental process, our Spiritual Consciousness becomes inactive, allowing us to learn, train, till, grow, and sow back into the Kingdom of God using our Gifts, Calling, Talents, and Creativity. In addition, it is also designed to prepare us according to our Divine Blueprint or Spiritual Assignment.

What if we do not have a Spiritual Assignment? We all have one. If not, we would NOT be here. We have just forgotten the Spiritual Assignment, replacing it with our own agenda. Why would we forget about what God sent us to do? We are NOT Spiritually Conscious of it as of yet. Please do not feel bad; it happens to us all. It is a part of the Spiritual Process for our Heaven on Earth Experience.

I went through this Spiritual Awakening Process, feeling my way through and stubbing my toe occasionally, but here we are. Therefore, if one follows my lead, I can place a Spiritual Guarantee or Seal on it, them, or us. How can I place guarantees as such? First and foremost, I am Spiritually Commissioned to do what I do. Secondly, I know what I am talking about without pulling for straws or filling the gap with fluff. And thirdly, I have spent years on the backside of the desert training for a time such as this. It was NOT EASY, nor do I wish the training upon anyone...but it is well worth it!

Above all, know this: God will TRAIN one person to train another with a multiplier effect, removing the trial-and-error hiccup and replacing it with knowledge, understanding, instructions, know-how, how-to, and Divine Wisdom. As I live by example, if we approach people, places, things, and events *As It Pleases Him*, we can become humbly better than the Spiritual Teacher, doing more extraordinary things. Really? Yes, really!

Through my BATTLE SCARS, I Spiritually Secure the ARMOR of the next man, leaving no stone unturned. Although we are all different with unique Spiritual Blueprints, my job is INCOMPLETE if I have not trained well, laid the finite groundwork, and helped to get us in Purpose on purpose with the Spiritual Tools needed to make our better best, good great, and average excellent. What makes this so important? We need to know what to do and be Spiritually Conscious when the enemy is in the camp, when he has unleashed a yoke, or when he is trying to antagonize our Bloodline. So, let us go deeper...

When reestablishing the connection to our Spiritual Consciousness, *As It Pleases God*, we must defrag our character. What does defragging have to do with anything? We must eliminate the negative, debauched, or ungodly traits or fruits we have picked up. How can we build good character, *As It Pleases God*? Regardless of where we are on our Spiritual Journey, when dealing with character, here are the basics:

- ☐ Know God's Word. By reading, studying, meditating, and applying God's Word, we can learn what pleases or displeases Him. We can also discover His Divine Principles and Spiritual Commands for every aspect of life.

- ☐ Pray. Prayer is how we communicate with God and express our love, gratitude, praise, confession, requests, and intercession. By praying regularly and sincerely, we can align our Mind, Body, Soul, and Spirit with God's Divine Will, growing in intimacy with Him.

- ☐ Obey. By obeying God's Word and His Spirit, we can show our loyalty and devotion to Him and become more like Him.

- ☐ Serve. By serving God and others with humility and joy, we can demonstrate our character and reflect His character.

- ☐ Repent and Forgive. By repenting of our sins, forgiving, and turning to God, we can receive His Divine Mercy and Grace and restore our fellowship.

These are basic ways to build good character, *As It Pleases God*. However, building character requires intentional effort and surrendering to God's Divine Will, aligning with our Predestined Blueprint. In addition, going to the next level of development involves being honest with oneself, recognizing one's weaknesses, and seeking God's guidance and strength to overcome them.

Building character, *As It Pleases God*, is a lifelong journey requiring consistency, perseverance, hope, faith, patience, proactiveness, and a strong work ethic. As relational beings, possessing good character traits such as honesty, integrity, kindness, and empathy, we are likelier to build trust with others and maintain healthy relationships, even when dealing with difficult people. Understandably, we are all different with varying people skills; therefore, someone must put in more internal work. So, it may as well be YOU!

Additionally, having a strong sense of character can help us make better choices and navigate difficult situations with grace and compassion. Listed below are a few tips on how to do so, but not limited to such:

- ☐ **Define Your Values and Principles**: Knowing what you stand for is the foundation of building good character.

- ☐ **Practice Self-Discipline**: It is one of the keys to building the inner man. Additionally, it is also one of the Fruits of the Spirit, assisting in developing good habits and avoiding temptation.

- ☐ **Embrace Challenges**: There are hidden treasures within challenges, providing growth opportunities for the Mind, Body, Soul, and Spirit. To thrive, As It Pleases God, you should embrace them, learn from them, use them to build resilience, and positively share your experiences with others.

- **Assume Responsibility**: Unbeknown to most, Accountability is Heaven's SECRET CURRENCY. Becoming accountable for your actions, reactions, thoughts, beliefs, and decisions, or the lack thereof, while learning from your mistakes, mishaps, or shortcomings, allows the Well of Divine Wisdom to flow on your behalf.

- **Cultivate a Positive Mindset**: Maintaining positive thoughts, inner chatter, or mental pictures will help you overcome obstacles, manifest good fruits, and create a win-win out of everything and with everyone.

By understanding these five character development tips, *As It Pleases God*, we can get down to the nitty-gritty. Why must we get down to the nitty-gritty when we are who we are? First, we are who we believe we are, correctly or incorrectly. Secondly, we must remove the negative, unproductive, and unfruitful layers of debris to bring forth our true selves. Thirdly, developing our way without God leads to justification, rationalization, lies, a cycle of déjà vu, and aborted missions.

Soul-searching is integral to character development, *As It Pleases God*, even if we think we do not need it. Why? It allows us to understand our motivations, desires, fears, and flaws. Thereby, we become authentically believable, relevant, and relatable. Exploring our internal world and examining our past experiences, thoughts, feelings, emotions, traumas, conditioning, and biases gives us the leverage to confront ourselves without sugarcoating, player-hating, or oppressing.

Why is our believability necessary, especially when we do not owe it to anyone? The hidden unsurety and cover-up make our story real or fake, depending on who tells their side. Therefore, we must give our Spiritual Fruits a VOICE to speak for themselves. As we develop our character and fruits, *As It Pleases God*, there are certain things we WILL NOT do, regardless of who tells their side of the story.

Here are the MOST DOMINANT character flaws negatively impacting our relationships, goals, happiness, success, or Divine Blueprint, but not limited to such:

- ☐ **Arrogance**: A sense of superiority, pride, or disdain for others.
- ☐ **Greed**: An excessive desire for wealth, power, or material possessions.
- ☐ **Envy**: A resentment or covetousness of what others have or achieve.
- ☐ **Wrath**: A tendency to engage in anger, rage, or violence.
- ☐ **Lust**: An uncontrollable craving for sexual gratification or pleasure.
- ☐ **Gluttony**: An overindulgence in food, drinks, or other substances and desires.
- ☐ **Cowardice**: A fear of facing danger, pain, or difficulty.
- ☐ **Dishonesty**: A habit of lying, cheating, or stealing.
- ☐ **Stubbornness**: A refusal to change one's mind, attitude, or behavior.
- ☐ **Impulsiveness**: A lack of forethought, planning, or self-control.
- ☐ **Jealousy**: A fear of losing someone or something belonging to us to a rival or foe.

- ☐ **Insecurity**: A lack of confidence, self-esteem, or trust in oneself or others.
- ☐ **Selfishness**: A disregard for the needs, feelings, or interests of others.
- ☐ **Perfectionism**: An unrealistic or obsessive standard of excellence or performance.
- ☐ **Negativity**: A pessimistic, cynical, or critical outlook in words, actions, deeds, thoughts, desires, or reactions.
- ☐ **Dependence**: A reliance on someone or something for support, guidance, or validation.
- ☐ **Indecisiveness**: A difficulty making choices, decisions, selections, or commitments.
- ☐ **Hypocrisy**: A contradiction between one's words and actions.
- ☐ **Vengefulness**: A desire to harm or retaliate against someone who has wronged us.
- ☐ **Impulsiveness**: A trait that can sometimes lead to hasty decisions without adequately considering the consequences.
- ☐ **Procrastination**: The act of delaying, postponing, or impeding a task or decision, often resulting in unnecessary stress and missed opportunities.
- ☐ **Laziness**: The unwillingness or lack of motivation to perform tasks or activities requiring effort or energy, often leading to unproductivity and missed opportunities.
- ☐ **Lack of Empathy**: A trait characterized by an incapability or unwillingness to understand or share the feelings of others, often leading to interpersonal conflicts and difficulty in building meaningful relationships.

- ☐ **Overthinking**: The tendency to dwell on a problem or situation for an extended period, often resulting in analysis paralysis and increased stress and anxiety.
- ☐ **Lack of Accountability**: The failure to take responsibility for one's actions or decisions, often resulting in a culture of blame-shifting and a lack of trust within a team or organization.
- ☐ **Impatience**: The tendency to become easily frustrated or irritated by delays or obstacles, often leading to impulsive decisions and a lack of attention to detail.
- ☐ **Competitiveness**: The desire to outperform others in a given task or activity, often focusing on winning rather than personal growth or collaboration.
- ☐ **Self-Depreciation**: The act of belittling oneself or one's abilities, often resulting in a lack of self-confidence and negative self-talk, hindering personal growth and success.
- ☐ **Self-Destruction**: The deliberate or unintentional actions that harm oneself physically, emotionally, or mentally, often resulting from a lack of self-worth or unresolved trauma.
- ☐ **Martyrdom**: Playing the victim or the blame game. Sacrificing one's needs or desires for the sake of others results in resentment or burnout if not balanced with self-care, healthy boundaries, and upright motives.
- ☐ **Rebellion**: An act of defiance, offense, or resistance against authority, often to overthrow or challenge the established order. It can take many forms, from peaceful protests to violent uprisings. Throughout history, rebellions have been a means for expressing dissatisfaction with the status quo and demanding change. While some rebellions have successfully achieved their goals, others have been crushed by

those in power, leaving a legacy of oppression, struggle, and Generational Curses.
- ☐ **Disobedience**: The act of intentionally disregarding or violating a rule, law, or command.

Why is anger not on the list? We all will experience anger at some point; however, it is derived from one or more of the most dominant character flaws. The same applies to fear, hate, trauma, and injustice.

Unfortunately, most may not recognize their flaws, cover them up, or choose not to deal with them, but they do not dissipate on their own. Why? They are seeds, lying dormant! They are developing a rooting system to bear fruit in due season as we face the consequences in our personal, professional, and Spiritual lives. What is the big deal, especially when no one is perfect? Perfection is not what God is looking for; He wants us to become a work-in-progress, working on ourselves from the inside out, not from the outside in.

Regardless of what life has served us, our character flaws can be overcome using the Fruits of the Spirit, awareness, a little effort, living by example, learning from others, and a Spiritual Mirror, *As It Pleases God*. If we dare to put on the *Whole Armor of God*, piece by piece, we can protect ourselves from ourselves. What does this mean? We often blame the enemy or someone else for what we are going through when it is NOT an outside source ailing us; it is the enemy from within, hidden in our psyche.

Character flaws can be minor, major, or tragic, depending on the severity and consequences of the flaw; plus, we all have them. How do we determine the difference to ensure we are not majoring on the minor? First, we must get an understanding of whatever with whomever, *As It Pleases God*, and not what pleases us. Secondly, we need Spiritual Discernment. And thirdly, we must know what the Word of God has to say about it, them, that, or us.

For example, here is what we must know about character development: "*And this I pray, that your love may abound still more and more in knowledge and all discernment, that you may approve the things that are excellent, that you may be sincere and without offense till the day of Christ, being filled with the fruits of righteousness which are by Jesus Christ, to the glory and praise of God.*" Philippians 1:9-11. Although this Spiritual Decree is hidden in plain sight, putting on the Whole Armor of God, using the Fruits of the Spirit, and behaving Christlike in a constant state of repentance, *As It Pleases God*, will UNVEIL the veiled.

As we go deeper, minor character flaws are usually harmless quirks or habits that do not cause much harm to others or oneself. For example, a person might be forgetful, clumsy, or stutter when anxious. Then again, it can include being overly critical, impulsive, picky, or indecisive. These idiosyncrasies might annoy or frustrate us, but they will NOT likely ruin one's life or happiness unless we make them major or tragic. Nevertheless, balancing these flaws with positive traits ensures our character does not become unlikable, selfish, or one-dimensional.

Major character flaws are more severe and often result from a lack of self-awareness, self-control, or empathy. For example, a person might be selfish, arrogant, rude, dishonest, or violent. Then again, some may struggle with anger management issues, while others grapple with jealousy, envy, pride, selfishness, coveting, or dishonesty. These flaws can cause significant harm to the individual and those around them, leading to strained relationships, poor decision-making, and a lack of fulfillment.

Individuals must recognize and address their character flaws to live a healthy, satisfying life, *As It Pleases God*. Why? These flaws can damage one's reputation, career, or relationships, requiring Spiritual Intervention, rehabilitation, therapy, mentored counseling, self-reflection, mindfulness, consciously changing negative behaviors, and using the Fruits of the Spirit to overcome.

Tragic character flaws are the most extreme and often lead to our downfalls or setbacks, similar to the events surrounding King Saul in 1 Samuel. Unfortunately, tragic flaws are usually rooted in a deep psychological wound or trauma we struggle to overcome. Then again, it can also stem from being disobedient, unrepenting, rebellious, disrespectful, or having a stiff neck, making a person paranoid, obsessive, vengeful, or suicidal. These flaws can drive us to commit terrible acts or make fatal mistakes, destroying our lives and those of others.

Regardless of our category, all hope is not lost; the Holy Trinity, the Fruits of the Spirit, and the *Whole Armor of God* are at our beck and call. All we need to do is USE them, *As It Pleases God*, with a work-in-progress mentality for the greater good. Here is the desired mentality when perfecting our character: *"But I want you to know, brethren, that the things which happened to me have actually turned out for the furtherance of the gospel, so that it has become evident to the whole palace guard, and to all the rest, that my chains are in Christ; and most of the brethren in the Lord, having become confident by my chains, are much more bold to speak the word without fear."* Philippians 1:12-14.

Building character is crucial to personal growth and development in the Eye of God; however, it is not a mandate. While it is not easy, it is doable.

- ☐ It requires commitment, effort, and sacrifice.
- ☐ It involves facing challenges, overcoming obstacles, and resisting temptations.
- ☐ It entails making mistakes, admitting faults, and seeking forgiveness.
- ☐ It demands growth, change, and transformation.

Amid all, this journey is rewarding, bringing peace, joy, and fulfillment, honoring God, blessing others, and glorifying Him. Here are ways to build character, but not limited to such:

- ☐ Be honest and trustworthy in all your interactions.
- ☐ Take responsibility for your actions and learn from your mistakes.
- ☐ Show empathy and kindness towards others.
- ☐ Practice patience and understanding, especially in difficult situations.
- ☐ Be a good listener and communicate effectively.
- ☐ Show respect to everybody, regardless of their status or position.
- ☐ Be self-disciplined and have a strong work ethic.
- ☐ Embrace challenges and learn from them.
- ☐ Practice gratitude and appreciate the good things in life.
- ☐ Be humble and avoid arrogance.
- ☐ Set goals and work towards achieving them.
- ☐ Be resilient and bounce back from setbacks.
- ☐ Show courage and be willing to take risks.

- ☐ Practice forgiveness and let go of grudges.
- ☐ Be open-minded and willing to learn from others.
- ☐ Be reliable and follow through on your commitments.
- ☐ Have a positive attitude and outlook on life.
- ☐ Show generosity and help others whenever possible.
- ☐ Be authentic to yourself.
- ☐ Continuously strive to advance, thrive, and grow as a person.

How can this list help us? First, we must want to be helped. Secondly, we must understand how we are created. And thirdly, we must understand our known or unknown needs. What if we had everything we needed? Congratulations! Now, my question is, 'Are you meeting the needs of another?'

We all have wants, needs, and desires hidden within our DNA, causing us to do what we do, say what we say, think how we think, and so on. The goal is to determine what drives our behavioral needs as a whole. What is the purpose of understanding needs, especially when we know what they are? They are encoded in our DNA, affecting how we perceive the world, interact with others, and cope with challenges. More importantly, they are the source of our passions, fears, hopes, and dreams, connecting us to our Predestined Blueprint or barring us from it.

Every human being has a few needs that they strive to fulfill throughout their lives:

- ☐ **Physiological**: Our physiological needs are the most basic and essential for life. They include food, water, air, shelter, clothing, sleep, and health. Without these needs, humans cannot function properly and may face serious health risks or even death. Therefore, satisfying these needs is the first priority for any human being.

- ☐ **Safety**: Our need for safety involves external protection from harm, danger, or threat. They include personal, financial, health, and environmental security. These needs help humans feel safe and secure in their surroundings and avoid anxiety and fear.

- ☐ **Certainty**: The need for stability and surety from within. Fulfilling the need for internal certainty can lead to a sense of peace, stability, and predictability, reducing stress and anxiety. In addition, it helps to build our faith, hope, and belief in who we are and why we are here.

- ☐ **Variety**: The need for adventure, excitement, and change. Fulfilling the need for uncertainty and variety can lead to excitement, adventure, and creativity, stimulating personal growth and development.

- ☐ **Significance**: The need for recognition, achievement, and importance. Fulfilling the need for significance can lead to a sense of accomplishment, recognition, and self-worth, boosting self-confidence and motivation.

- ☐ **Social**: The need for intimacy, affection, and relationships with others. Fulfilling the need for love and connection can lead to deeper relationships, emotional support, and a sense of belonging, improving overall well-being and happiness.

- ☐ **Growth**: The need for personal development, learning, and progress. Fulfilling the need for growth can lead to personal development, learning, and progress, increasing self-awareness and fulfillment.

- ☐ **Contribution**: The need to give back, help others, and positively impact the world. Fulfilling the need for contribution can lead to a sense of purpose, meaning, and impact, elevating one's sense of fulfillment and well-being.

- ☐ **Self-Actualization**: The innate desire of individuals to realize their full potential and achieve personal growth. Self-actualization involves the pursuit of goals that are aligned with one's values, interests, and strengths. It is a journey of self-discovery requiring introspection, self-reflection, and a willingness to take risks and learn from experiences. When individuals achieve self-actualization, they experience a sense of bliss, fulfillment, purpose, or meaning.

- ☐ **Touch**: The power of touch is truly remarkable. It can convey love, comfort, and support in ways that words cannot. A simple hug or a gentle touch on the hand can make someone feel cared for and valued. Research has shown that touch can have Mental, Physical, Emotional, and Spiritual benefits, such as reducing stress and anxiety, lowering blood pressure, boosting the immune system, and building trust or faith. It is incredible how such a simple gesture can profoundly impact our well-being.

All of these needs are interrelated and influence each other. How so? If a person lacks food or water (physiological need), they may be unable to focus on their work or education (self-actualization need). Similarly, if a person lacks social support or love (social need), they may feel depressed or hopeless (certainty need), putting their personal safety in danger.

One example of a hidden desire is the need for approval. This need is when we seek validation from others, whether it is through praise, recognition, admiration, or acceptance. We may not realize how much we depend on external feedback to feel good about ourselves, and we may sacrifice our authenticity or integrity to please others. The need for approval can stem from low self-esteem, insecurity, fear of rejection or abandonment, or past experiences of criticism or neglect.

Another example of a hidden desire is the fear of success. This need is when we sabotage our achievements or opportunities because we fear the consequences of success. We may fear that success will change us, alienate us from others, create more pressure or expectations, or expose us to envy or criticism. The fear of success stems from a lack of confidence, self-worth, trust in ourselves or others, a belief we do not deserve happiness or fulfillment, or unresolved trauma.

A third example of a hidden desire is the longing for connection. This need is when we crave meaningful relationships through friendships, romance, family, or community. We may not admit how lonely or isolated we feel and may avoid or reject opportunities to connect with others. This longing for connection can stem from a lack of social skills, emotional intelligence, empathy, or compassion, or a history of trauma, abuse, loss, or betrayal.

We must be honest and explore our feelings and motivations to uncover and manage them. We can also seek professional help from a therapist, coach, mentor, or counselor if we need guidance or support. By understanding and accepting our hidden desires, we can make better choices that align with our true selves and highest potential.

Fulfilling our needs in this manner can lead to a more balanced life with a sense of purpose, connection, and personal growth. Even if we pretend we do not have needs, we do! Even if we pretend we cannot be satisfied, we can! Regardless of how we adapt and cope, we have basic human needs to help us become better, stronger, and wiser, living healthy, joyful, happy, and meaningful lives.

What if we DO NOT know our wants, needs, or desires? It is okay...it happens to us all, but the psyche knows; it is just playing hide and seek. Here is the deal: To uncover your wants, needs, desires, or Divine Blueprint, you can start by reflecting and meditating on what truly matters to you. Not anyone else, what matters to you! Then, ask yourself questions and document the answers.

- ☐ What makes me happy?
- ☐ What displeases me?
- ☐ What are my passions and interests?
- ☐ What do I value most in life?
- ☐ What are my long-term goals?
- ☐ What are my short-term goals?
- ☐ What do I want to achieve in my personal and professional life?
- ☐ What are my biggest passions in life?
- ☐ What motivates me to get up in the morning?
- ☐ What are my greatest fears?
- ☐ What are my strengths?
- ☐ What are my weaknesses?

- ☐ What makes me feel fulfilled?
- ☐ What are my favorite hobbies?
- ☐ What are my biggest regrets in life?
- ☐ What is my definition of success?
- ☐ What is my definition of failure?
- ☐ What are my priorities in life?
- ☐ What are my biggest challenges?
- ☐ What challenges me the least?
- ☐ What do I want to be remembered for?
- ☐ What are my ideal living conditions?
- ☐ What is my ideal career?
- ☐ What do I want to achieve in life?

Why must we document? Your answers may change periodically. For this reason, it is WISE to keep up with the changes to measure our growth. My answers 20 years ago do not match my present-day answers. Reflecting from then to now motivates me to keep moving in the Spirit of Excellence regardless of how life seems or what I have going on.

In addition, you can also try journaling your thoughts at a specific time each day, talking to a trusted friend, hiring a coach, or engaging in activities that bring you joy and fulfillment. Pay attention to your emotions and physical sensations, as they can often provide clues to what you really want and need. Remember that self-discovery is an ongoing journey, so be patient and kind to yourself as you explore your inner world. *"Therefore if there is any consolation in Christ, if any comfort of love, if any fellowship of the Spirit, if any affection and mercy, fulfill my joy by being like-minded, having the same love, being of one accord, of one mind. Let nothing be done through selfish ambition or conceit, but in lowliness of mind let each esteem others better than himself. Let each of you look out not only for his own interests, but also for the interests of others."* Philippians 2:1-4.

Can query journaling really change us? Absolutely! On the other hand, if we opt not to question ourselves or journal the answers, *As It Pleases God*, it could devastate us Mentally, Physically, Emotionally, or Spiritually. How? When we do not have a reference point or Testimony documented, we judge others immensely, forgetting about our journey, where we came from, or our destination, zapping our Spiritual Reflective Measures. Listen to me, and listen well: There is a big difference between bringing the Good News with documented evidence, word-of-mouth hearsay, and pulling for straws.

Spiritual Reflective Measures

Experience is the best teacher known to man, yet LOST, unlearned, or undeveloped experiences are still the greatest downfall. With your Spiritual Reflective Measures, there is someone who can learn from you amid your goodness, badness, or indifference. My question is, 'What do you do with it or them?' Do you:

- ☐ Hoard.
- ☐ Judge.
- ☐ Bury.
- ☐ Share.

We have the Bible because someone knew the value of Spiritual Documentation. With *The WHY Blueprint*, I do not want only to HEAR your journey; I want to SEE it documented as a TESTAMENT of your faith. I am sharing these questions for you to query yourself...just do it and document it, and your story will come forth.

Back in the day, there was a young man named Reggie, who heard about the importance of building good character, but paid it no attention. He arrogantly believed he could handle any temptation on his own, his money could buy his way out of anything, and he did not need to buy into Spirituality or Religion. He thought the Spiritual Hoopla was unnecessary, feeling that all Believers were wimps, simps, or broke pimps according to his standards.

One day, he faced a complex situation, testing his faith, integrity, and every word sown in and out of season. Instead of relying on God, he used his strength, money, and knowledge without Divine Wisdom to handle the situation, continually throwing his weight and title around to feed his ego.

While playing like God Almighty to pacify himself, he fell into plaguing temptation, leading to negative consequences. He lost a job he worshipped, endured a failed relationship with his fiancé, who ran off with the maintenance man, sued for a large sum of money that wiped out his life savings, and became sterile. As God completely severed his Bloodline, he realized a few things too late. They were:

- ☐ He should have invested in working on his character.
- ☐ He should have trusted in his Heavenly Father a little more instead of putting all his duckies in one basket.
- ☐ He should have avoided defaming the Kingdom of God for selfish gain.
- ☐ He should have respected others instead of insulting them for not having what he possessed.

And now, Reggie is mad at the world and God, playing the victim, and still doing his own thing, tapping into all types of alternative Religions to coax the hidden pain and looking for a quick fix. However, he learned that relying on his strength and money was insufficient, especially when his Bloodline stopped with him.

As a result of knowing the TRUTH and willfully operating in the mindset of disobedience, he is treading the fence, having one foot in the Kingdom and one foot out, like he is fooling God. While simultaneously thinking all Believers are like him, projecting this negativity onto others, until he met me.

Reggie considered my kindness a weakness and soon realized I was not down for the okey-doke, refusing to accept his folly and mangled fruits as my portion. However, he tried to break me down with mind games and reverse psychology, similar to what he does with others. This old-school player failed to realize I was a humble STUDENT, operating with the Fruits of the Spirit and in Divine Purpose.

As the Heavenly of Heavens would have it, he was TRAINING me with this informative STORY to give back to the Kingdom for a time such as this. Why? There were two different mindsets at play here:

1. **Mindset One**: I will break her down, proving she is not who she says she is. She is just like the rest of them; she is too weak to be stronger than me.

2. **Mindset Two**: I am going to get this story. I am going to get this story. I am going to GET IT! Lord, I am the one for the job; who can tell it better than me?

Regardless of our mindsets, opting for the story to feed God's sheep, *As It Pleases Him*, is never a bad idea; it is the BEST. However, attempting to outsmart God, destroy a Divine Vessel He uses to feed His sheep, or abort the Predestined Blueprint of someone who is in Purpose on purpose is UNWISE! Why? Operating in selfishness to prove our stats without Spiritual Discernment will invoke the Plagues of Egypt to fall upon us or our Bloodline.

What if we are not in Egypt, having free will to do whatever, whenever, and however? Even if we operate in freedom, it does not exempt us from the consequences of our choices, even if we think we are in control or have it going on. The Plagues of Egypt represent a condition or an invoked circumstance associated with our MINDSET.

Reflectively speaking, when manipulating, conniving, and scheming, if we use deceptive measures, we had better ensure our intended targets are NOT operating with the Fruits of the Spirit and Christlike Character, or engaging in their Blueprinted Mission, *As It Pleases God*. Why should we exercise extreme caution for those under the Wing of God or His Watchful Eye? According to the Heavenly of Heavens, a Spiritual Vessel operating in such a manner is Spiritually Guarded with a deflective SHIELD and SEAL. Our ill-willed attempts may backfire or cause a damaging leak within the human psyche, potentially contaminating our Bloodline in due time.

In any case, we SHOULD NOT play around with innocent lives, especially without Spiritual Discernment. Notably, when engaged in debaucherous efforts or uncorrected and unaddressed rotten fruits lying all over the place, we build our own nesting edifices. For this reason, I do not condone playing games with the lives of others.

But for those who are hell-bent like Reggie on playing with rotten fruits, it is best to play with others with fruits of a like kind. Why? When dealing with the Fruits of the Spirit, we play by a different set of Spiritual Rules. We should not engage if we do not know the difference between good and bad, right and wrong, just and unjust, positive and negative, and so on. Why? They will get us caught up in the Vicissitudes of Life on a cycle of déjà vu with unrecognizable, mangled fruits. For this reason, *Spirit to Spirit*, do not leave home without loading up on the Fruits of the Spirit; they work in or out of season, regardless of how life appears to the naked eye.

Outsmarting God should never become our method of operation, especially when dealing with the lust of the eyes, the lusts of the flesh, and the pride of life. Why is this such a Spiritual Taboo? Without repentance, they will cause us to turn on ourselves without realizing we are our worst enemy. How is this humanly possible? The internal enemy is manifested through our thoughts, words, actions, reactions, biases, beliefs, and judgments. What about the external enemies? No one can become our enemy if we do not allow them to get into our heads with doubt and negative mental chatter. In the Eye of God, they are designed to become our footstool or Spiritual Classroom, preparing and training us for the next level. Really? Yes, really! "The Lord said to my Lord, '*Sit at My right hand, Till I make Your enemies Your footstool.*'" Psalm 110:1.

According to our Predestined Blueprint, we can overcome our enemies from the inside out with our FAITH in God and OBEDIENCE to His Divine Will. How is this possible, especially when we have issues? Our *Spiritual Reflective Measures* make them subservient to our Divine Mission without realizing it, while they think they are getting over or winning.

To think we are winning and winning in the Eye of God is like apples and oranges in the Kingdom. What is the difference between them? Thoughts are fleeting with no need for substance and sustainability; they are a free-for-all, requiring no rhyme or reason. Whereas operating with a winning mindset, *As it Pleases God*, is proactive and progressional, keeping us on a positive, productive, and fruitful learning curve, developing the Fruits of the Spirit and our Christlike Character.

No one is exempt from negative, doubtful, or deceptive seeds; when we think we are, we will 'get got' by our internal critic. Here is the deal: Initially, the enemy is designed to shoot his shots, provoking wrath and division. Secondly, it is our responsibility to cast them down or counteract them with positivity, the Word of God, wise affirmations, the Fruits of the Spirit, and ONENESS. Thirdly, it does not mean we should become divided, even if people are divided amongst themselves.

Everyone must do their part in connecting to the Spiritual Objective of ONENESS, contributing their piece to the puzzle. If someone chooses not to become a part of it, it is their free will to exempt themselves from their portion. Nor should we place false expectations on them. Unfortunately, the false expectations we set for others instigate disappointment within us, causing the psyche to act up, go haywire, or receive mixed signals.

How can we operate in ONENESS amid division? We must remain in a state of repentance, forgiveness, love, peace, humility, and perseverance to exude the sovereignty hidden in all things, making us better, stronger, and wiser. More importantly, we must tap into our Divinely Blueprinted Mission or our reason for being. When we move in the right direction, *As It Pleases God*, it comes with a protective cloud by day and a pillar of fire by night, guiding us to our PROMISE. Really? Yes, really!

Divine Inclusion

When we are in Purpose on purpose, *As It Pleases God*, we have the Divine Right to invoke Spiritual Pillars, be it by cloud or smoke; whatever we need, we can DECLARE and DECREE it. Is this Biblical? I would have it no other way, *"And the Lord went before them by day in a pillar of cloud to lead the way, and by night in a pillar of fire to give them light, so as to go by day and night."* Exodus 13:21. Are we exempt from using this Spiritual Principle because it is in the Old Testament? We are exempt if we believe we are. Then again, we can remain in contempt for not using the Spiritual Tools that are readily available.

As for me and my Bloodline, I want all that belongs to us; therefore, I claim Divine Inclusion. How do we claim Divine Inclusion? All we need to do is Spiritually Consecrate ourselves to our Heavenly Father, cover ourselves with the Blood of Jesus, allow the Holy Spirit to guide us, and do what we were sent here to do in the first place.

We have the same Spiritual Authority that Moses possessed; however, we must know how to tap into it without tapping out. Surrendering our Spiritual Power to an ungodly governing authority with the potential of mass manipulation and destruction is an insult to the Kingdom of God. For this reason, we must know and understand God for ourselves with a *Spirit to Spirit* Relationship. By disrespecting those He placed in charge or projecting ill will as a form of retaliation will eventually cause us to shake in our boots, letting us know the man-made or erected walls will come down.

Even King David knew, in the Eye of God, it was an abomination to take King Saul out; therefore, he had to RESPECT him, even though David disagreed with his method of operation. For those who think it is cool to insult those who God has IN CHARGE, let me break it down in Kingdom Terminology. The same SWORD we use as our tongue is used to judge our house, so BEWARE! Blasphemy, right? Wrong.

As God has given us Spiritual Dominion, there are Spiritual Rules of Engagement for a person IN CHARGE and one who is NOT! This Spiritual Principle applies to Believers and non-believers alike...here is the SPIRITUAL WARNING **Saith the LORD**:

"Now it happened afterward that David's heart troubled him because he had cut Saul's robe. And he said to his men, 'The LORD forbid that I should do this thing to my master, the LORD's anointed, to stretch out my hand against him, seeing he is the anointed of the LORD.' So David restrained his servants with these words, and did not allow them to rise against Saul. And Saul got up from the cave and went on his way. David also arose afterward, went out of the cave, and called out to Saul, saying, 'My lord the king!' And when Saul looked behind him, David stooped with his face to the earth, and bowed down. And David said to Saul: Why do you listen to the words of men who say, 'Indeed David seeks your harm?' Look, this day your eyes have seen that the LORD delivered you today into my hand in the cave, and someone urged me to kill you. But my eye spared you, and I said, 'I will not stretch out my hand against my lord, for he is the LORD's anointed.' Moreover, my father, see! Yes, see the corner of your robe in my hand! For in that I cut off the corner of your robe, and did not kill you, know and see that there is neither evil nor rebellion in my hand, and I have not sinned against you. Yet you hunt my life to take it. Let the LORD judge between you and me, and let the LORD avenge me on you. But my hand shall not be

against you. As the proverb of the ancients says, 'Wickedness proceeds from the wicked.' But my hand shall not be against you." 1 Samuel 24:5-13.

Our agenda versus God's Agenda cannot be overlooked, downplayed, or manipulated, even if we have cheated through the system our whole lives. For this reason, we must stop playing with Spiritual Governing Orders we do not understand. If one thinks they are exempt from how David handled this Spiritual Matter, let me be the first to say, 'We are NOT!'

According to the Ancient of Days, the same Spiritual Rules applied back then to a man after God's own heart apply to us right now. Why? We have gotten out of control with the vehicles of disrespect. When we cannot respectfully and rationally think for ourselves, discerning between right and wrong, our Spiritual Signals or Arrays from the Heavenly of Heaven can get mixed up or develop mangled interferences.

What does one thing have to do with another? Once again, we are Spiritual Beings having a human experience. If we cannot RESPECT who is in charge in the earthly realm, we will DISRESPECT the Heavenly, even if we proclaim to love God with all our heart, mind, and soul. What if we do? I am not judging the level of love; I am determining if one is fit for the Kingdom Accolades, Wisdom, Treasures, Secrets, Promises, or the UNVEILING of our Divine Blueprint.

In the same way, the Children of Israel wandered in the desert for forty years for ungratefulness and disrespectfulness; we are subjected to the same occurrence, even if we love and adore God. What does this mean? We have a choice:

- ☐ Divine Inclusion.
- ☐ Divine Exclusion.

Why must we choose between being included and excluded? When dealing with *The WHY Blueprint*, we must know what includes and excludes us in Kingdom Privileges. God will not open up the Kingdom of Heaven only to have us spit in His face because we cannot get what we want or manipulate Him as we please. When representing the Kingdom, if we cannot relate to our Heavenly Father personally using our people skills and the Fruits of the Spirit, *As It Pleases Him*, our Spiritual Levels will remain low in our vibrational efforts.

For example, we can love God with all our hearts, speaking highly of Him. Still, we cannot lift our voices to break a yoke. We are clueless about contending with the enemy's wiles, deflecting the truth about our situation, or spreading rotten and mangled fruits among our brethren. While simultaneously treating people like junkyard dogs or spreading untruths because of underlying jealousy, envy, pride, greed, coveting, competitiveness, or debauched alliances. Do we think God is pleased with this mess? Absolutely not! So, why are we begging for the Keys to the Kingdom without doing a checkup from the neck up? God is here for us all, but we must step up our game at some point.

What are the repercussions of NOT knowing the difference between positive and negative, good or bad, right or wrong, just or unjust, and so on? Not knowing the difference comes with Spiritual Woes and Blinders. Overlooked or misunderstood woes create blockages within the psyche and conscience, creating all forms of stress and disease. Can this really affect us? Absolutely! *"Woe to those who call evil good, and good evil; who put darkness for light, and light for darkness; Who put bitter for sweet, and sweet for bitter!"* Isaiah 5:20.

We become internally confused without God because *"Every way of a man is right in his own eyes, but the Lord weighs the* hearts." Proverbs 12:2. If we do not add God into our equational efforts, Spiritual Correction cannot fully occur, *As It Pleases Him*. Why can it not occur if we are believers? If we are on a cycle of déjà vu, we will continue this pattern until we make a CONSCIOUS decision to step into the Spiritual Classroom for a character overhaul or pruning. Why will we remain in this cycle? *"For My thoughts are not your thoughts, Nor are your ways My ways," says the Lord. For as the heavens are higher than the earth, So are My ways higher than your ways, And My thoughts than your thoughts."* Isaiah 59:8-9. For this reason, a *Spirit to Spirit* Connection must be developed for Divine Alignment to occur.

We all have the freedom to choose our paths and make decisions based on our free will, but it is always beneficial to seek and follow Spiritual Guidance, *As It Pleases God*. When dealing with Divine Order, we can take it all the way to the left; however, when dealing with God Almighty, we must reel it in according to His Divine Word, Spiritually Tilling our own ground. What does this mean? We must want it for ourselves...no one can do this for us!

In *Divine Inclusion*, we CANNOT take our Spiritual Alignment for granted. Why? Being in harmonious ONENESS with the Holy Trinity and our Divine Purpose is a sought-after state of being for all mankind, filling the hole in us with HOLINESS. Spiritually Syncing ourselves in this manner can be achieved through prayer, repenting, fasting, forgiving, meditation, self-reflection, living in accordance with the Word of God, and suiting up with *The Whole Armor of God*. By doing so, we experience a sense of internal peace, joy, purpose, and fulfillment, and we can navigate life's challenges with greater ease, favor, mercy, and grace.

CHAPTER FIVE
Blueprint Hindrances

When understanding our *WHY Blueprint*, we must comprehend it from God's Divine Perspective, *As It Pleases Him.* How do we gain a Divine Perspective when we are of flesh and blood and have real issues? We all have issues, but they DO NOT make us Kingdomly unusable unless we develop deaf ears, have stiff necks, or operate in a Spirit of Rebellion. Although we can talk about this until I am blue in the face, let me break this down into layman's terms. Proverbs 16:6-19 says, These six things the LORD hates, Yes, seven are an abomination to Him:

- ☐ A proud look.
- ☐ A lying tongue.
- ☐ Hands that shed innocent blood.
- ☐ A heart that devises wicked plans.
- ☐ Feet that are swift in running to evil.
- ☐ A false witness who speaks lies.

- And one who sows discord among brethren.

If one has not noticed, the things God hates will snowball into each other, becoming a complete mess with time. How? When we are too proud, we lie, stretching the truth until it loses its elasticity, or sheds innocent blood. To keep our shenanigans going, we put on masks, devise plots, plan debauchery, falsely represent ourselves, and sow discord to keep our image alive. More importantly, when the snowball appears, it is fully grown and engrafted within our psyche and Bloodline.

With *The WHY Blueprint*, it is our reasonable service to share how we can become entangled in our own web of deception while appearing right in our own eyes. By becoming aware of what we are doing and why, we can understand our thoughts, character, and behaviors before getting a side-eye from God Almighty.

Proud Look

When speaking of a proud look, we often do not see a problem with looking proud from a human perspective. For example, when working on something or someone, we want to be considered a proud parent, child, student, author, or whatever. On the other hand, from a Divine Perspective from the Heavenly of Heavens, a proud look looks differently in the Eye of God. How does it look different? Lacking humility makes everything and everyone appear different in the Eye of God. Why? It is a watered-down version of disobedience.

Unbeknown to most, obedience is required when it comes down to *The WHY Blueprint* because God has the Divine Instructions we need to receive. If our communicative channels are blocked by disobedience, rebellion is on the horizon, even if we pretend to be masters at controlling ourselves. Simply put, if God is NOT in our self-control, it is limited by our triggers, habits, and traumas. What is the purpose of knowing this? The Fruits of the Spirit are designed strategically to help us balance our triggers, habits, and traumas.

Suppose we do not use or know anything about the Fruits of the Spirit: Love, Joy, Peace, Patience, Kindness, Goodness, Faithfulness, Gentleness, and Self-Control. In this case, our fleshly character supersedes our Christlike Character. Unfortunately, this is why Believers put their paws on others while making excuses for misbehaving in the Name of God. Then, they deflect the blame with lies to cover up their actions without telling the truth about being consumed with jealousy, envy, pride, greed, coveting, and competitiveness.

For the record, just because we are tithing does not justify violating another person, nor does it give us a license to do so. God would prefer that we keep our tithes rather than disrespect His sheep or use social media to defame or bring shame to someone's name. If someone thinks their tithing gives them discernment, another Spirit is at play, causing them to play themselves short in the Eye of God and man. The bottom line is that if we are proud to harm another, Mentally, Physically, Emotionally, Spiritually, or Financially, we must check our heart posture because our eyes are haughty.

How do we know if we are battling with haughty eyes or a proud look? All we need to do is check our fruits, behaviors, thoughts, responses, words, or biases. What if we do not know what to check for? Here are a few items, but not limited to such:

- ☐ Are you rolling your eyes at people as a response?

- ☐ Are you giving them a side-eye when you know they are right?
- ☐ Are you responding negatively to someone or something without just cause?
- ☐ Do you think you have all the answers, needing no correction?
- ☐ Do you place yourself above people to feel superior?
- ☐ Are you very critical of everything or anyone?
- ☐ Is it hard for you to say, 'Please, Thank you, Excuse me, or I am sorry?'
- ☐ Do you argue all the time?
- ☐ Are you disrespectful?
- ☐ Are you ungrateful?
- ☐ Are you genuinely happy for others?
- ☐ Are you bragging about yourself or your possessions all the time?

Although this list is not set in stone, it will give us an idea of what to look for, allowing us to self-correct, self-query, and self-align, *As It Pleases God*.

Lying Tongue

Using lying as a pastime has become our modern-day entertainment, which is highly frowned upon in the Kingdom of God. Why? Although sometimes entertaining for those with itchy ears, lies are seeds, serving us our portions in due time; therefore, we do not want to engage in something or with someone we cannot disengage from. Lies have hidden yokes, eventually consuming us.

What if we are not a liar? What if I say, 'That is a lie?' For example, we do not need to teach a child how to lie; it is already embedded within them. Now, it is our responsibility as parents to teach them otherwise, including self-correcting our own lies.

If we think we are exempt from lies, we are sadly mistaken and deceiving ourselves. Here is the deal: the human psyche naturally lies, so we need self-correction, self-control, and repentance to tame the fiery lies. Without them, the hidden secrets under the lies will cause an implosion or explosion when triggered or shaken to the core. Here is how to recognize our internal lying tongue, but not limited to such:

- ☐ Do you avoid telling the truth about your role in a situation, circumstance, or event?
- ☐ Do you hide your wrongdoings by exposing someone else's?
- ☐ Are you a master at deflecting the truth or telling half-truths?
- ☐ Are you withholding vital information from someone who could benefit from it?
- ☐ Are you very two-faced, hypocritical, or playing with a third face (mask)?
- ☐ Do you battle with exaggeration of the facts to get attention?
- ☐ Are you very misleading with your actions, thoughts, beliefs, or words?
- ☐ Do you use the truth against someone to break them down or expose them?
- ☐ Do you intentionally set traps for people to fall into to discredit them?
- ☐ Do you have an issue with keeping your word or commitments?
- ☐ Do you constantly make excuses?
- ☐ Do you blame others for your behavior?

Self-correcting ourselves with the Fruits of the Spirit requires involving the Holy Trinity. Why must we involve the Holy Trinity? It allows our conscience to provoke or nudge us amid our wrongdoings. For those who think the conscience is a figment of our imagination...it is not. It connects to our Spiritual Compass, guiding, prompting, and alerting us through our natural senses. What does this mean? Our conscience sometimes uses what we can instantly relate to, such as our ability to see, smell, hear, taste, and touch, to warn us.

Innocent Blood

Our conscience is a complex system working with our five senses to help us make decisions. How is this possible? Our conscience processes the information we receive through our senses and gives us a sense of right and wrong, good or bad, positive or negative, just or unjust, and so on. When we make choices going against our values, our conscience may send feelings of guilt or shame to alert us that we are acting against our beliefs. More importantly, the conscience lays dormant if we DO NOT have values or morals, leaving us to our own devices with an unscrupulous mindset and shedding innocent blood.

What is shedding innocent blood, especially if we are not hurting anyone physically? It is wrapped in the thoughts, behaviors, words, beliefs, and biases projected upon one another. Here are a few ways to shed innocent blood, but not limited to such:

- ☐ Yelling, screaming, fussing, and fighting with others.
- ☐ Exhibiting anger, hatred, or rudeness to others.
- ☐ Bullying or manipulating others for our benefit.

- ☐ Excluding others from our circle.
- ☐ Carelessly abusing and hitting someone to inflict pain or for control.
- ☐ Gossiping to degrade others negatively.
- ☐ Criticizing, lying, or name-calling.
- ☐ Belittling, insulting, or disrespecting others.
- ☐ Discriminating against others.
- ☐ Betraying or throwing others under the bus.
- ☐ Stealing from others to benefit ourselves.
- ☐ Cheating on someone or trying to beat the system.

These behaviors can have severe consequences and can deeply hurt those around us. Cultivating a kind and empathetic attitude toward others and treating them with respect and dignity is essential to keep our conscience intact, *As It Pleases God*.

Can the conscience abandon us? It does not abandon us; we abandon the conscience by not using, ignoring, or suckerpunching it. The moment we repent, begin using the Fruits of the Spirit, and behave Christlike, *As It Pleases God*, it will awaken to serve as a Spiritual Compass. What about the Holy Trinity? Our conscience works outside of the Holy Trinity because God loves us all and will always give us tools to help ourselves, even if we do not choose to use the Holy Trinity or care less about the Father, Son, and Holy Spirit.

On the other hand, when it comes to our Divine Blueprinted Purpose, this is where the limits are drawn. Our Predestined Blueprint can only be UNVEILED along with the Holy Trinity (Father, Son, and Holy Spirit). Why? It is Spiritually Guarded, similar to the Garden of Eden in the Book of Genesis, with Spiritual Principles, Laws, and Protocols.

Now, for those who think they DO NOT need Spiritual Principles, Laws, and Protocols to tap into their Predestined Blueprint, it is fair for me to say that they have not tapped into their FULL POTENTIAL yet. How can I say such a thing, especially when someone is highly favored and has it going on? We can have all the above without being in Purpose on purpose, knowing nothing about our reason for being, and cannot hit a lick at a crooked stick!

If we take off the masks, remove the crutches, and go toe-to-toe, building our lives from the ground up, one-on-one with God Almighty, it will show us what and who we are working with and the lies we inadvertently tell ourselves. For this reason, it behooves us to use the Spiritual Principles, Laws, and Protocols to help us on our Spiritual Journey. What makes this so important? We are Spiritual Beings having a human experience. If we do not know this, life has a way of teaching us before it is over and done.

In the Eye of God, having power, money, sex, beauty, or influence does not replace our Divine Blueprint. There will always be a longing for more of this and more of that as ungratefulness becomes our portion. When all we need to do is change our MINDSET to *As It Pleases God*, use the Fruits of the Spirit, behave Christlike, repent daily, and think positively—everything else will take care of itself. What about the Holy Trinity (The Father, Son, and Holy Spirit)? It is always best to take one step at a time; if we begin with these few steps, they will make a Believer out of us.

When living with clean hands and a pure heart, *As It Pleases God*, our conscience gives us inner peace, balance, and satisfaction. And if or when our peace is broken or an imbalance occurs, it puts us on high alert or gives us red flags that something is not right or a person does not match our soulish vibes, causing us to tread with extreme caution. When doing so, know this: *"The truthful lip shall be established forever, But a lying tongue is but for a moment."* Proverbs 12:19. When operating in integrity, it changes the rules of the game, As It Pleases God, even if the liar appears to have the upper hand.

How do we know if we are straddling the fence with our lies and conscience? It will vary from person to person, situation to situation, culture to culture, and bias to bias. Remember, everyone appears right in their own eyes with a sliding scale perspective, leaning toward ourselves. Nevertheless, here are a few items to watch for, but not limited to such:

- ☐ Lying to others or ourselves.
- ☐ Cheating on tests, in games, or in relationships.
- ☐ Stealing from others or trying to beat the system.
- ☐ Ignoring our responsibilities.
- ☐ Hurting others with our thoughts, words, beliefs, behaviors, or actions.
- ☐ Engaging in gossip that has nothing to do with us or spreading rumors.
- ☐ Failing to help someone in need.
- ☐ Refusing to apologize when we are wrong.
- ☐ Ignoring the needs of our loved ones.
- ☐ Being selfish, self-centered, or manipulative.
- ☐ Ignoring or neglecting ourselves or the well-being of others.
- ☐ Disrespecting authority or the law.
- ☐ Failing to stand up for what is right.
- ☐ Engaging in negative, harmful, or addictive behaviors or habits.
- ☐ Being unfaithful in our relationships, friendships, parenting, or with commitments.
- ☐ Ignoring our values, principles, or beliefs of righteousness.

- ☐ Blaming others or pointing the finger for our own mistakes.
- ☐ Engaging in unethical personal or business practices.
- ☐ Discriminating against others based on race, gender, or other factors.
- ☐ Failing to learn from our mistakes or refusing to grow as individuals.

Even if we think lies do not affect the conscience, they do! It also affects our *Spirit to Spirit* Relations with our Heavenly Father. How? Suppose we go before God, pleading the Blood of Jesus and asking for the presence of the Holy Spirit without repenting for smacking someone in the face because the opportunity presented itself. Do we think the Rod of Correction will not apply to us? It will apply more to us because we should have known better.

Devises Wicked Plans

If we are walking around bragging about negative behavior, making a name for ourselves without Spiritual Correction, rest assured, the conscience has not fully kicked in. Shedding innocent blood is not what God expects from us, especially when jealousy, envy, pride, greed, coveting, and competitiveness are involved. When we point the finger or play the victim, we must realize we may not be so innocent; therefore, we must check our thoughts, beliefs, motives, words, actions, reactions, and conscience.

How would we conduct a Spiritual Mirrored checkup based on our thoughts, beliefs, motives, words, actions, reactions, and conscience? We must query ourselves because the psyche will hide things from us so that we can play the victim without becoming victorious. Listed below are a few questions to ask yourself, but not limited to such:

- ☐ What were your thoughts at the time?
- ☐ What were your beliefs about the situation, circumstance, or event?
- ☐ What were your motives? Were they biased?
- ☐ What were you talking about? Why were you speaking about this?
- ☐ What were your actions at the time? How were you behaving? What were you doing at the time?
- ☐ How did you react? Were you playing the victim? Were you manipulating the situation?
- ☐ What did your conscience reveal to you? How did you feel about whatever?
- ☐ What did you do to reverse engineer this to create a win-win?

Why does God use our conscience as a Spiritual Compass in our *Spirit to Spirit* Relations? He created the Mind, Body, Soul, and Spirit to work together as ONE, *As It Pleases Him*. Once we use them as He rightly intended, they will take care of each other. For example, when our thoughts are not right, they will be felt in other areas. If our psyche is unkempt, it will signal other areas that something is wrong, or we will feel a void. Since we are all different, there is no cookie-cutter approach; we need the conscience as a Spiritual Compass, helping us pinpoint the lie, trauma, trigger, void, or whatever.

As a word to the WISE, we are designed to read the Spiritual Compass to determine the Spiritual Antidote.

Why do we need a Spiritual Compass, especially when qualified to diagnose an individual? A human diagnosis differs from a Spiritual One; we need both to create balance. Why? If we have a worldly individual dealing with a Spiritual Matter of oppression, they need to be Spiritually Grounded. If not, there could be a Spiritual Transfer.

For example, when dealing with electrical devices, we must have a grounding wire as a safety measure to prevent power surges, short circuits, or fires. Unfortunately, we are no different; Spiritual Grounding is needed to deal with the unexpected distractions designed to get us off track. Our degrees and certifications cannot handle Spiritual Matters, and if one is not Spiritually Equipped to deal with both, they should refer the case to someone who deals with both.

When playing around in the Realm of the Spirit without proper authority, we can become a not-so-innocent victim because we should have listened to our conscience and referred the case to a Spiritual Practitioner. What is the big deal? Those who take on cases they cannot handle are subjected to the same thing because they have too many open doors (unresolved or unrepentant issues). Unfortunately, this is why many psychiatrists need a personal psychiatrist to cover up or get through what they have unawaringly picked up. Why would this happen, especially when doing their job? Once again, their ego would not allow them to let go of a case when their conscience told them otherwise.

For example, once an actor takes on an evil role, they must Spiritually Purge it from their system; if not, the negative characteristics remain attached to them. The human psyche does not know the difference between real and imagined; it goes on what it is being fed and the connectivity factor. In the Realm of the Spirit, energy is energy, positively or negatively. As a human SPONGE, we will absorb it, making repelling and repenting important for all humanity.

Running To Evil

Now, getting back to us, if we do not know our point of erring or what we need to repent, how can healing occur with Spiritual Blinders, Deaf Ears, and a Muted Voice? Unfortunately, we cannot heal what we do not admit or what we cover up with something else. Since we are not born with a compass, is this Biblical? Of course, this is Biblical, and we are born with a conscience as a Spiritual Compass that cannot be seen as tangible but felt intangibly through our senses. What makes this so important in the Eye of God is, *"Can the blind lead the blind? Will they not both fall into the ditch?"* Luke 6:39. Without using our Spiritual Compass, *As It Pleases God*, we will fall short by default, even if we appear to stand tall.

We are designed to help pinpoint what is broken or rusty, allowing the Holy Spirit to fix the hole in us, ensuring we are calibrated, *As It Pleases God*, and not as it pleases ourselves. On the other hand, due to our free will, if we desire to please ourselves, then we must do our own calibrating without the Spiritual Benefits of the Holy Spirit.

In the self-calibration process, we develop feet that are swift in running to evil, plotting revenge, turning our noses up, conspiring negatively, or developing a maskful cover-up. All in all, pleasing ourselves will cause the Holy Spirit to lie dormant.

Is the Holy Spirit not for everyone? Yes, He is available to all, but we must become ONE with Him in humility, not disobedience. Playing with the Holy Ghost FIRE is a quick way to get placed six feet under while still alive. What does this mean? The psyche will begin to do a number on us, causing inner turmoil from the inside out; therefore, due to the Blood of Jesus, He (The Holy Spirit) lays dormant until we are ready.

Our Spiritual Compass must work to keep our Kingdom Status as a Spiritual Elite. Here is what we need to know to ensure our Spiritual Compass is up to par and on point, but not limited to such:

- ☐ God uses our conscience to convict us of sin and lead us to repentance.
- ☐ Our conscience is an ethical compass guiding us toward righteousness and astuteness.
- ☐ God uses our conscience to bring us comfort and peace in times of trouble.
- ☐ Our conscience helps us discern the Will of God in difficult situations.
- ☐ God uses our conscience to warn us of danger or potential harm.
- ☐ Our conscience helps us make wise decisions that align with God's plan for our lives.
- ☐ God uses our conscience to prompt us to show the Fruits of the Spirit to others and to behave Christlike.
- ☐ Our conscience helps us recognize and resist temptation.
- ☐ God uses our conscience to reveal areas of our lives needing Spiritual Growth, Maturity, Regrafting, or Pruning.
- ☐ Our conscience helps us remain accountable to our faith, hope, and commitment to God.
- ☐ God uses our conscience to inspire us to pursue justice and righteousness.
- ☐ Our conscience helps us cultivate a deeper understanding and relationship with God.

- ☐ God uses our conscience to challenge us to step out on faith and trust while Spiritually Tilling our own ground.
- ☐ Our conscience helps us recognize and acknowledge our limitations and weaknesses, allowing us to become a work-in-progress.
- ☐ God uses our conscience to prompt us to seek forgiveness and reconciliation with ourselves and others.
- ☐ Our conscience helps us navigate complex relationships and conflicts.
- ☐ God uses our conscience to bring healing and restoration to the brokenness in our lives, causing *The WHY Blueprint* (What Hurts Us is What Heals Us) to work on our behalf.
- ☐ Our conscience helps us recognize and appreciate the beauty and goodness of God's Divine Creation and Nature.
- ☐ God uses our conscience to encourage us to live in Purpose on purpose.
- ☐ Our conscience helps us experience the fullness of God's Divine Grace and Mercy.

When dealing with our conscience, we cannot take a lying tongue lightly, nor should we leave it as-is, unrepented, uncorrected, or unreversed engineered. With *The WHY Blueprint*, lies become a quick way to shed innocent blood without realizing it until after the fact. So, we must continuously filter our Mind, Body, Soul, and Spirit with the Word of God with positive thoughts, actions, reactions, and words.

Most ask, 'What was so special about King David, especially with a flawed track record?' Could it be that his feet were not swift at running to evil? Could it be that he was willing to correct his conscience, *As It Pleased God*? Could it be that He knew the Voice of God and obeyed it? No one truly knows besides God, right? However, David left us with enough information to glean.

God rewards obedience, courage, and humility with a work-in-progress mentality. David never stopped working on himself; he was locked in on becoming stronger, wiser, and more astute daily without settling for defeat. When genuinely dedicated to the Kingdom of God, our heart posture becomes laser-focused on what pleases God while quickly repenting over our hiccups. According to *The WHY Blueprint*, let us look at WHY King David was after God's Heart.

- ☐ David sincerely believed in God Almighty, trusting His plan without reservation.
- ☐ He repented, asking for forgiveness when he sinned and seeking proactive forgiveness not to sin.
- ☐ David was dedicated to prayer, worship, and his *Spirit to Spirit* alone time with God.
- ☐ He was very obedient, even when it was difficult.
- ☐ David showed mercy and kindness to his enemies, even though He had a lot of blood on his hands and would take a man out at the drop of a dime.
- ☐ He was very caring for the people of God.
- ☐ David had a heart for justice, integrity, and righteousness.
- ☐ He understood his need for God's help and guidance amid his imperfections.
- ☐ David was a man of courage and bravery, doing what needed to be done.

- ☐ He deeply loved God's Word, meditating on it day and night.
- ☐ David had a humble and reasonable heart with a willingness to serve others, even as a King.
- ☐ He trusted in God's provision and protection.
- ☐ David was a man of vision and creativity.
- ☐ He left a legacy of faith and devotion to God, documenting his encounters.
- ☐ David was a man of wisdom who sought to understand God's ways.
- ☐ He was a man of humility who recognized his weaknesses and shortcomings.
- ☐ David was a man of compassion who proactively cared for the needs of others.
- ☐ He was a man of loyalty who remained faithful to God and his people.
- ☐ David was a man of love who demonstrated God's love to others.
- ☐ He was a man of vision who saw beyond the present circumstances to God's plan.
- ☐ David was a man of creativity who used his talents and abilities for God's glory.
- ☐ He was a man of leadership who inspired others to follow God.
- ☐ David was a man of generosity who gave generously to God's work.
- ☐ He was a man of gratitude who thanked God for His Divine Blessings.
- ☐ David was a man of hope who trusted in God's promises for the future.
- ☐ He was a man of patience who waited on God's timing.
- ☐ David was a man of peace who sought to resolve conflicts in God's way.

- ☐ He was a man of joy who celebrated God's goodness.
- ☐ David was a man of perseverance who endured trials and hardships.
- ☐ He was a man of purity who sought to live a HOLY life before God.
- ☐ David was a man of justice who sought to right wrongs in God's way.
- ☐ David was a man of unity who brought people together for God's purposes.
- ☐ He was a man of determination who never gave up on God's plan.
- ☐ David was a man of understanding who discerned God's will for his life.
- ☐ He was a man of encouragement who lifted others up in their faith.
- ☐ David was a man of boldness who stood up for God's truth.
- ☐ He was a man of faithfulness who remained loyal to God and his people.
- ☐ David was a man of holiness who pursued righteousness before God.

By no means was King David perfect, but his good outweighed his bad. And the same applies to us. Our good deeds must carry Spiritual Weight to supersede the dead weight of our imperfections, weaknesses, or shortcomings. Therefore, in your Spiritual Journal, make sure you document your good and bad deeds. Why? Awareness is one of the keys to God's Divine Heart, and cluelessness is a lock.

False Witness

Bearing false witness is the act of making a false statement about someone or something to cause harm or damage to their reputation, mindset, or credibility. Spreading rumors or false information about others is a seed in the Eye of God, bearing fruit in due season.

Sowing discord among our brethren will cause us to become responsible for the domino effect caused by what we willingly set in motion to destroy one person. What does this mean? The seed we sow affects one person and then affects another, and so on. Every person it affects, directly or indirectly, we are held accountable in the Eye of God, positively or negatively. Therefore, it behooves us to keep our seeds positive, productive, and fruitful.

What if we are locked in on the negative? We had better make sure our target is negative, behaving like us. Why must we focus on the negative instead of the positive? It takes one person to know WHO and WHY they are in the Eye of God with positive fruits and character, *As It Pleases Him*, to cause a negative seed or intent to backfire. Once it does, it can target anything and anyone associated with us. So, we should never play around like this, especially when we have children.

Bearing false witness can negatively affect how we relate to ourselves and others, impacting our *Spirit to Spirit* Relations with our Heavenly Father. Here are a few consequences of bearing false witness in the Eye of God, but not limited to such:

- ☐ Damage to one's reputation.
- ☐ Loss of trust and credibility.
- ☐ Legal consequences, such as fines or imprisonment.
- ☐ Blaming others or pointing the finger for our issues.

- ☐ Ruined relationships.
- ☐ Loss of employment or job opportunities.
- ☐ Alienation from friends and family.
- ☐ A battle with anger, guilt, revenge, or anxiety.
- ☐ Decreased self-esteem and self-control.
- ☐ Increased stress levels.
- ☐ Loss of respect for ourselves and from others.
- ☐ Decreased ability to make sound judgments.
- ☐ Loss of integrity and honor.
- ☐ Negative impact on future opportunities.
- ☐ Loss of respect for the justice system.
- ☐ Negative impact on the community.
- ☐ Damage to institutions that rely on trust.
- ☐ Increased conflict and division within the psyche.
- ☐ Decreased sense of responsibility.
- ☐ Negative impact on one's spiritual or moral beliefs.

In *The WHY Blueprint*, we must MASTER the ability to ask fact-finding questions or fact-check instead of reverberating untruths or half-truths. When doing so, we cannot knowingly interject false propaganda to satiate our agenda, further our motives, or bring shame to someone's name. Then again, often, we fall short because we aim to trip someone up to cater to what we want to hear, what we desire, or based on a false expectation. Bearing false witness is more about being a master manipulator.

What is a manipulator? A manipulator uses their skills, experience, or knowledge to influence or control a situation or person deceptively or unfairly. This effort can be done through lying, withholding information, or using emotional manipulation. It is essential to be aware of manipulators and their tactics to protect oneself from being taken advantage of, Mentally, Physically, Emotionally, Spiritually, or Financially.

Why do we become manipulators? The reasons will vary from person to person, situation to situation, or culture to culture; however, most will become manipulators based upon power, money, and sex, stemming from jealousy, envy, pride, greed, coveting, competitiveness, or some form of corruption within the human psyche. What if we are not a manipulator for any of these reasons? In this case, we must check our level of trauma, negative habits, unhealthy thoughts, soul ties, and superfluous words relating back to our cultural patterns stemming from the lust of the eyes, the lust of the flesh, and the pride of life.

Manipulators are experts at using language to influence, regulate, and perpetuate. They often use persuasive language and subtle cues to manipulate their targets into doing what they want, when they want it, and how they want it. For example, they may use flattery or charm to gain someone's trust and then gradually introduce ideas serving their own interests. They may also use veiled threats or insinuations to make their targets feel guilty or ashamed. Then again, they can also use vague language to keep them confused, controlled, or off-balance.

Ultimately, manipulators are skilled at using language to get what they want, often without the other person realizing what is happening. It is essential to be aware of these tactics and to avoid falling prey to them. If you are not sure if you are being manipulated, here are a few indicators, but not limited to such:

- ☐ You feel confused and unsure of yourself or another person.

- ☐ Your opinions and beliefs are constantly questioned or dismissed.
- ☐ You feel guilty or ashamed for expressing your thoughts, feelings, and perspective.
- ☐ The other person tries to control your behaviors, thoughts, beliefs, or decisions.
- ☐ You feel like you are walking on eggshells around them.
- ☐ The other person uses guilt, anger, or fear to get what they want.
- ☐ They isolate you from friends and family.
- ☐ You feel like you are constantly apologizing or making excuses for their behavior.
- ☐ They make you feel like you owe them something.
- ☐ The other person constantly criticizes, ignores, dismisses, belittles, or cuts you off.
- ☐ They make you feel like you are always in the wrong, and they are right.
- ☐ The other person uses emotional manipulation to gain control.
- ☐ They gaslight you, making you doubt your own perceptions, thoughts, and memories.
- ☐ You feel like you are never good enough.
- ☐ The other person uses passive-aggressive behavior to get their way.
- ☐ They make you feel like you are responsible for their happiness.
- ☐ You feel like you are sacrificing your own needs and desires for the other person.
- ☐ The other person uses flattery or charm to manipulate you.
- ☐ They make you feel lucky to have them in your life.
- ☐ You feel like you are constantly giving but never receiving in the relationship.

Throughout my Spiritual Journey, I have found that most manipulators do not realize they are manipulating people, places, and things to get what they want. How could they not know? Once this Jezebel Spirit (manipulating and scheming) becomes a part of our character, it operates like algae taking over a body of water, depleting the oxygen, and creating toxic conditions.

Who is Jezebel? Jezebel is a Biblical figure known for her wickedness and manipulation in 1st and 2nd Kings. She was the wife of King Ahab and sought to promote the worshipping of false gods, assassinating prophets who opposed her beliefs, and contending with God Almighty, leading to this husband and wife duo's downfall. Some of her defining characteristics include her pride, arrogance, and willingness to use her power for personal gain at the expense of others.

What does Jezebel have to do with us now? The Spirit of Jezebel is still amongst us, doing what it does best. More importantly, we think Jezebel is just about women, but I beg to differ. Male or female, the character traits of the Jezebel Spirit deplete our good works, love, service, faith, and most of all, patience. Blasphemy, right? Wrong. *"I know your works, love, service, faith, and your patience; and as for your works, the last are more than the first. Nevertheless I have a few things against you, because you allow that woman Jezebel, who calls herself a prophetess, to teach and seduce My servants to commit sexual immorality and eat things sacrificed to idols. And I gave her time to repent of her sexual immorality, and she did not repent. Indeed I will cast her into a sickbed, and those who commit adultery with her into great tribulation, unless they repent of their deeds."* Revelation 2:19-22.

Playing one person against another is not what God has in mind for us; He wants us to REPENT. When we are divided

The WHY Blueprint

or intentionally divide others, unity is placed on the back burner.

A name with a complicated history, as Jezebel, there are also misunderstandings involved. Most think the Jezebel Spirit is all bad, negative, and evil, but it is not. God wants us to reverse engineer her behaviors to create a win-win for ourselves without wiping out our Bloodline. The bottom line is that the MINDSET of the Jezebel Spirit will determine our stepping stones or brick walls.

For example, *The WHY Blueprint* is predicated on 'What Hurts You is What Heals You.' If you learn, grow, and sow back into the Kingdom based upon the Law of Reciprocity and *As It Pleases God*, it changes the trajectory of the intentionality of the Jezebel Spirit. On the other hand, if you DO NOT learn, grow, and sow, *As It Pleases God*, only to please yourself, then instead of creating a stepping stone to the next level, you erect a brick wall blocking your progress until you repent and glean what you need to learn. Listed below are a few ways to reverse engineer bearing false witness or avoid being manipulated by a Jezebel Spirit, but not limited to such:

- ☐ Place God first in your life, according to His Divine Will.
- ☐ Be aware of your thoughts, emotions, fears, and desires, allowing the Holy Spirit to help you self-correct.
- ☐ Remain calm in challenging situations, exhibit self-control, and cover yourself in the Blood of Jesus.
- ☐ Always question the source of information and check for credibility, testing the Spirit, As It Pleases God.
- ☐ Do not allow fear or guilt to dictate your decisions.
- ☐ Do not be swayed by persuasive language or emotional appeals.

- ☐ Avoid making decisions based on incomplete information or half-truths.
- ☐ Take the time to think through and pray about a situation before reacting.
- ☐ Do not be afraid to ask questions and seek clarification, learning from everything and everyone.
- ☐ Be aware of your biases and evaluate from multiple perspectives.
- ☐ Do not be pressured into making a decision quickly.
- ☐ Stay vigilant and be wary of anyone who tries to rush you.
- ☐ Look out for signs of manipulation, such as flattery, fast-talking, or excessive praise.
- ☐ Trust your instincts; do not ignore red flags or violate your conscience.
- ☐ Be skeptical of anyone who tries to isolate you from others.
- ☐ Do not be afraid to say no and set boundaries.
- ☐ Surround yourself with supportive and trustworthy people.
- ☐ Do not be afraid to seek help or advice from others.
- ☐ Practice positive assertiveness while confidently standing up for yourself.
- ☐ Remember, you have the power to make your own decisions respectfully.

Sowing Discord

As we live, we face all types of people, places, and things designed to get our attention. Once gained, good or bad seeds can be sown to manipulate or cater to the psyche, positively or negatively. Unfortunately, due to our unawareness, discord is sown more than harmony.

How do we sow discord? There are many different tactics used to emit discordance with negative seeds. But what is more unraveling is when someone throws rocks and hides their hands as if they have done nothing wrong. Listed below are a few character traits associated with the Spirit of Discord, but not limited to such:

- ☐ Mockery
- ☐ Stirring the pot
- ☐ Coveting
- ☐ Competitiveness
- ☐ Jealousy
- ☐ Envy
- ☐ Resentment
- ☐ Selfishness
- ☐ Pride
- ☐ Arrogance
- ☐ Stubbornness
- ☐ Negativity
- ☐ Gossiping
- ☐ Lying
- ☐ Manipulation
- ☐ Insensitivity
- ☐ Greediness
- ☐ Dishonesty
- ☐ Rudeness
- ☐ Disrespectfulness
- ☐ Narcissism
- ☐ Condescension
- ☐ Judgementalism
- ☐ Unforgiveness

When sowing discord, most do not realize they are engaging in such acts, causing God to give them a side-eye. How can we avoid sowing discord? We must change our MINDSET, *As It Pleases God*. If not, we will develop a stiff neck by default without knowing we have a crook in it.

For example, if God has the mind, the body will eventually follow! On the other hand, if we take on the title without surrendering the mind, it leads to having a stiff neck. Really? Yes, really! Here is what we miss: *"Do not lift up your horn on high; Do not speak with a stiff neck."* Psalm 75:5. What about the mind? Our horn can be our mindset or our mouth; whether we have a stiff-necked mentality or mouth, it is all the same in the Eye of God. Of course, we do not walk around with physical horns, but our MINDSET horns remain with us, and are revealed through our actions, reactions, words, thoughts, beliefs, seeds, and fruits. Remember, the horns of an animal are never attached to any other part of the body except for the head; furthermore, if it is attached anywhere else, RUN!

Our strengths, power, weaknesses, or downfall lie in our MINDSET. We often choose our horn without realizing our choices due to the lack of understanding, *As It Pleases God*. Is this Biblical? I would have it no other way, *"All the horns of the wicked I will also cut off, But the horns of the righteous shall be exalted."* Psalm 75:10.

Having the Mind of Christ is not as difficult as most would think. All we need to do is align our thoughts, words, actions, and reactions with God's Divine Will, opening ourselves up to the Fresh Oil instead of a stiff neck.

CHAPTER SIX
Fresh Oil

Do you have a desire to become Spiritually Fresh? Do you long to have the Oil of Divine Glory? Do you have an urge to discern between freshness and staleness? The desire to carry Spiritual Oil from the inside out is a natural desire we all have, but we often fail to understand how to recognize it, get it to flow, or turn it off. As a result, we begin to wing it, hoping our Spiritual Oil becomes potent to show off to prove our worthiness. In the Eye of God, the Spiritual Oil or the Fresh Oil does not work for show; it works for results in Spiritual Growth, Development, and Alignment.

How do we get Fresh Oil? According to the Word of God, we must fill our horns with oil and go, using the Fruits of the Spirit, trusting His Divine Wisdom and Guidance as the Prophet Samuel did. Blasphemy, right? Wrong. For example, *"Then Samuel took the horn of oil and anointed him in the midst of his brothers; and the Spirit of the LORD came upon David from that day forward. So Samuel arose and went to Ramah."* 1 Samuel 16:13.

David possessed the criterias needed for the Fresh Oil to flow. How do I know? When Samuel used the horn to please himself based on looks and not Divine Instructions, the Fresh Oil would not flow, prompting God to say, "*Do not look at his appearance or at his physical stature, because I have refused him. For the LORD does not see as man sees; for man looks at the outward appearance, but the LORD looks at the heart.*" 1 Samuel 16:7.

When we are in Purpose on purpose, the Fresh Oil will flow; however, we can adapt to whatever or whomever, but when it comes down to Divinely Flowing, *As It Pleases God*, it will not happen. For this reason, we want Fresh Oil according to our Predestined Blueprint and not someone else's. Can we make such requests to God? Absolutely!

God prefers us to seek Him in all things. Why? We do this to avoid having the distressing Spirit of Saul follow us due to acts of disobedience, pompousness, and selfishness. What does this mean? If we do not take the time to learn, God will allow someone to learn from us to accomplish His Divine Will. Simply put, use what you have in your hands, or become the example God uses for not using what you have, as He causes your stale oil to become FRESH OIL for the next man.

How can our stale oil become fresh to someone else? A fresh mindset, *As It Pleases God*, turns rankness into freshness when using the Fruits of the Spirit and Christlike Character. For example, grapes must become crushed and fermented to get fresh wine, right? Now, depending on the length of the fermentation process, it defines fresh wine from fine wine, determining its VALUE.

Remember, some people live better than us by habit and are closer to God than those in God's face all the time with a mask, as if He cannot see them for who they are. I am referring to those who appear to do what is right but do wrong behind closed doors or when no one is looking. How can those close to God be far away from Him? Their habits, character, beliefs, and fruits contradict what He expects from Believers.

God is looking for our people skills. Is this Biblical? Of course, our people skills are referred to as the interests of others. *"Therefore if there is any consolation in Christ, if any comfort of love, if any fellowship of the Spirit, if any affection and mercy, fulfill my joy by being like-minded, having the same love, being of one accord, of one mind. Let nothing be done through selfish ambition or conceit, but in lowliness of mind let each esteem others better than himself. Let each of you look out not only for his own interests, but also for the interests of others. Let this mind be in you which was also in Christ Jesus, who, being in the form of God, did not consider it robbery to be equal with God, but made Himself of no reputation, taking the form of a bondservant, and coming in the likeness of men."* Philippians 2:1-7.

What about our personal relationship with God? Is He not concerned? Our relationship with Him is easy because we are Spiritual Beings having a human experience. On the other hand, dealing with ourselves and others creates issues within the human psyche.

Why is dealing with ourselves a problem? There is a war between our carnality and Spirituality (Flesh and Spirit), making it easy to put on our Religious face, but when facing ourselves and others, we have issues. If we do not know how to treat people right, we must ask ourselves, 'Are we treating the Father, Son, and Holy Spirit right behind closed doors?' 'Are we using the Holy Trinity properly?' 'Are we applying the Word of God in our lives?' 'Are we operating outside of the Word of God and taking it out of context to please ourselves or our agenda, tooting our own horns?' What is the purpose of these questions? They determine the freshness of our Spiritual Oil or the Divineness of our Spiritual Horn.

Fresh Oil and a Fresh Mindset, *As It Pleases God*, equate to a Divine Horn of Spiritual Connection, Significance, Power, and Reverence. What is the Spiritual Secret of our Divine Horns, Oils, or Mindsets? To be clear, everyone has access to the normal portions of human connection, respect, power, and significance, containing no sacredness; it is free for all. Whereas with all things Spiritual, we are held to a higher standard to partake of the many Spiritual Secrets hidden in plain sight outside of a Divine Miracle. What is the difference? A Divine Miracle can supersede Spiritual Laws to preserve or build our faith. On the other hand, with Spiritual Secrets, we must put in the work, doing our due diligence, *As It Pleases God*.

When we are trained with Spiritual Principles, not only do we receive Supernatural Miracles, but we can initiate them according to our Predestined Blueprint. When we are in Purpose on purpose, God's responsibility is to facilitate whatever is needed to further our Divine Mission. With this expectation, He will literally move Heaven and Earth to save us, but we must KNOW our reason for being and ALIGN accordingly.

Why must we KNOW and ALIGN, *As It Pleases Him*? Anyone or anything violating the Will of God for our lives, we have the Spiritual Right to cast it down or reject it or them, while covering ourselves with the Blood of Jesus. Really? Yes, really! Conversely, if we DO NOT know our reason for being, if we DO NOT have a *Spirit to Spirit* Connection with God Almighty, and if we DO NOT have Spiritual Discernment, we work against ourselves, casting down what God uses to process, purify, or regraft us. Can this really happen to us? Absolutely!

God has sent me on many assignments to feed His sheep, only to get rejected as if I were the enemy. So it is quite common to reject what He sends to nurture us, biting the hand sent to feed us. How did they miss it? They lacked Spiritual Discernment.

Instead of convincing them to receive from the Heavenly of Heavens, here again, I walked away with the STORY. For this reason, I will share the Secret POWERPLAYS, helping us to help ourselves, but not limited to such:

- ☐ **The First Secret**: We must fill our Spiritual Horns to pour out in the Spirit of Righteousness.

- ☐ **The Second Secret**: We must feed God's sheep at the prompting of the Holy Spirit, developing obedience.

- ☐ **The Third Secret**: We must cover our Mind, Body, Soul, and Spirit with the Blood of Jesus as Spiritual Atonement.

- ☐ **The Fourth Secret**: We must use the Fruits of the Spirit and Christlike Character.

- ☐ **The Fifth Secret**: We must positively counteract negativity to create a win-win.

- ☐ **The Sixth Secret**: We must repent and forgive without being easily provoked.

- ☐ **The Seventh Secret**: We must confidently move forward in the Spirit of Excellence, regardless of how life appears to the naked eye.

The Powerplay Secrets, *As It Pleases God*, creates a Well of Wisdom, overflowing its banks. Is this humanly possible? Of course, I am living proof.

Suppose you humbly follow my instructions, *As It Pleases God*. In this case, He will grant you information, concepts, and ideologies defying science. Plus, according to your Predestined Blueprint, He will give you what is set aside for ONLY you. If you do not believe it, repeat this for the next 40 Days if you desire the Fresh Oil to flow from your Divine Horn, *"But my horn You have exalted like a wild ox; I have been anointed with fresh oil."* Psalm 93:10.

If we operate our lives, *As It Pleases God*, He is in it with us. If we use the Fruits of the Spirit, He is in them. If we behave Christlike, He is a part of them too. When we repent, we release our flaws to Him. God is in all of them, allowing us to learn how to use our Spiritual Tools in the real world instead of staking a claim to the title of being a Believer, not knowing how to use what we have in our hands.

According to the Heavenly of Heavens, He prefers us to know how to use our Spiritual Tools before proclaiming the title. Why would God Almighty prefer this? When under a Spiritual Attack or in Spiritual Warfare, a title cannot help us; we need Spiritual Skills and Ammunition to reverse engineer the enemy's plan.

More importantly, we must know how to use the Blood of Jesus without misusing it. Blasphemy, right? Wrong. We are out of order if we use the Blood of Jesus before repenting. How so? This discourse is similar to taking a bath without getting in the water. We must repent (wash away) and then (call) using the Blood of Jesus to Spiritually Cover us. *"Arise and be baptized, and wash away your sins, calling on the name of the Lord."* Acts 22:16. *"Wash me thoroughly from my iniquity, And cleanse me from my sin. For I acknowledge my transgressions, And my sin is always before me."* Psalm 51:2-3.

Listen to me and listen well: When our Spiritual Fruits are pleasing in the Eye of God, when behaving Christlike, and locking in on a Positive Mindset, *As It Pleases Him*, we can take the Word of God, cover it with the Blood of Jesus, and invoke the Holy Spirit, using them to break any yokable or debilitating stronghold at the drop of a dime. More importantly, if we can do this, we do not need to tell anyone or anything about a title, denomination, status, or whatever; they will KNOW IT.

If you are challenged in any area, repeat this over and over until the Spirit of Peace comes over you: *"Purge me with hyssop, and I shall be clean; Wash me, and I shall be whiter than snow. Make me hear joy and gladness, That the bones You have broken may rejoice. Hide Your face from my sins, And blot out all my iniquities. Create in me a clean heart, O God, And renew a steadfast spirit within me. Do not cast me away from Your presence, And do not take Your Holy Spirit from me. Restore to me the joy of Your salvation, And uphold me by Your generous Spirit."* Psalm 51:7-12.

CHAPTER SEVEN
Reverse Engineer

Our lives are full of ups and downs, twists and turns designed to prepare us for the next level. However, our NEXT is predicated on our WHY, be it known or unknown, causing propellation or stagnation. Regardless of which one, it takes hard work, dedication, perseverance, and the same amount of energy. So, it behooves us to develop a positive mindset and *Reverse Engineer* our lives since we have to do the work anyway.

We are often taught to go with the flow or to deal with whatever, as if we do not have a say. Unfortunately, with *The WHY Blueprint*, we have a say and the Divine Right to stake our claim to what concerns us. How is this possible, primarily when life happens to us all? We have the right to leave it as-is or adjust our mindset to create a win-win by *Reverse Engineering* the trajectory of it, them, or that.

The *Reverse Engineering* process is taking something apart to understand how it works according to the original design, and making the necessary adjustments to improve. This process is designed to help us achieve our goals and dreams according to our Divine Blueprint, ushering in a better life for ourselves, our Bloodline, and the Kingdom of God, inspiring others to do likewise. If we choose not to use this manifestation process, we cannot blame anyone for not achieving our goals. Here are a few steps to *Reverse Engineer*, but not limited to such:

- ☐ Define your desired outcome. What do you want to achieve in your life? What are your values, passions, and goals? Be specific and realistic, and write your answers in your *WHY Blueprint* journal.

- ☐ Analyze your current situation. Where are you now concerning your desired outcome?

- ☐ What are your strengths, weaknesses, opportunities, and threats? What are the gaps and obstacles that prevent you from reaching your outcome?

- ☐ Break down your outcome into smaller steps. What are the milestones and actions that will lead you to your outcome? How can you measure your progress and success? How long will it take to complete each step?

- ☐ What can you learn from others? What can you learn from their strategies, mistakes, and advice?

- ☐ Experiment. Try different approaches and methods to achieve your desired outcome. Learn from your failures and feedback. Adjust your plan as you go along.

- ☐ Celebrate your achievements and enjoy the journey. Reward yourself for completing each step and reaching your outcome.

- ☐ Appreciate the process and the lessons you learned along the way. Share your results and insights with others.

The WHY Blueprint helps us become a positive and fruitful contribution to all, leaving a legacy of Divine Wisdom and Profound Impact. It is not about proving our doubters wrong but about keeping ourselves from the Spirit of Doubt, getting rid of our fears, and counteracting our limitations by exemplifying our FAITH through documentation.

According to the Heavenly of Heavens, your faith allows you to understand your WHY, making *'What Hurts You is What Heals You'* relevant and proactive. Meanwhile, doubt will cause *'What Hurt You to Hinder and Hate You,'* making you negatively reactive, angry, and disobedient. Nevertheless, regardless of where we are or what we have going on, we have the power to change the trajectory of our lives using *The WHY Blueprint*. Here is how:

The only person who can stop this process from occurring is YOU. How is this possible? The lack of knowledge, Spiritual Knowledge to be exact, is our greatest downfall. Our second greatest downfall is manipulating the system to take down another without just cause or throwing our weight around as if the Eye of God Almighty is not watching.

Remember, our actions, thoughts, beliefs, and biases are seeds, creating little seedlings in our own house; therefore, we must ensure they are positive, productive, and fruitful, *As It Pleases God*. If not, we can 'get got' by our own devices for power, money, and sex, derived from the lust of the eyes, the lusts of the flesh, and the pride of life.

From the south, where I am from, we have an adage saying, '*The spotlight will blind your headlights.*' Simply put, too much attention will blind you, boosting your ego to the reality of your next step or what is coming, like a deer blinded by a vehicle's headlights.

What if we have the perfect family? Perfection is a matter of perception. Clearly, I wish the best for every family, extending peace, joy, love, and happiness, but the lies must cease. We all will have something to work on to become better, stronger, and wiser, individually or as a family. If God is not at the forefront, I am sorry...I am not buying perfect! I buy into the work-in-progress family, removing the element of shame.

What does shame have to do with anything? Shame presents itself to those who put on imageable illusions, masks, and coverups. Conversely, the yoke of shame cannot penetrate those dedicated to working on themselves or their families, who understand the power hidden in *Reverse Engineering* the narratives to create win-wins.

How does this *Reverse Engineering* work? Suppose someone sows seeds of anger, resentment, discord, jealousy, envy, pride, greed, coveting, competitiveness, or debauchery. In this case, perfection is only a far-fetched illusion for this individual until self-correction occurs. Why? We must operate with the Fruits of the Spirit and Christlike Character with a work-in-progress mentality, Spiritually Tilling our own ground, *As It Pleases God*. If not, in due season, we will reap what we have sown, positively or negatively, from the inside out.

What can we do to help ourselves? *The WHY Blueprint* is designed to help us *Reverse Engineer* our hurts, pains, fears, failures, mistakes, jealousy, envy, hate, or setbacks into Divine Greatness, regardless of how it appears to the naked eye. How can this happen, especially when our lives are in a mess? Everything has a lesson attached, and if we learn how to ask the right questions, we can glean what we need and discard what we do not, building our skills, talents, and creativity to become the best version of who we are, *As It Pleases God*.

Living on our own terms, with the freedom to do, say, and become whatever we desire, is a coveted state of being. But we must also ask, 'Why are we not living the desired life?' 'Do we know how to do it?' 'Are we confident enough to pursue our dreams, desires, or hopes?' Regardless of our questions, we must also have a plan to achieve. *The WHY Blueprint* is not about figuring it out or making it up as we go; it is about PLANNING our way out of whatever with whomever.

Why must we plan, especially when we have it going on, needing nothing from anyone? Congratulations to those who have it going on. The average person with a family cannot just walk away from a job to pursue their dreams without considering their family's well-being. On the other hand, anyone can use their job to finance their dreams, hopes, passions, or interests and take care of their family simultaneously. How is this possible? *The WHY Blueprint* is how we can proactively plan to overcome obstacles and challenges from the inside out. What does this mean? We build the EMPIRE from within first, and then build the foundation of our heart's desires through the power of documentation.

If we are not good at the power of documentation right now, it does not mean we should not master our documentary power; WE SHOULD! It builds confidence in the assuredness of who we are without trying to be someone else or what defies our *Divine Blueprint*. In developing resilience, we may need a consultant, mentor, or coach to assist us on our Spiritual Journey to avoid chucking and jiving.

In building confidence, learning, and growing, *As It Pleases God*, we need clarity, focus, discipline, flexibility, patience, humility, and obedience. What if we omit them? Taking them for granted inadvertently interjects jealousy, envy, pride, greed, coveting, and disobedience into our lives. If we do not *Reverse Engineer* the negative into positive attributes and win-wins, they will remain, doing what they do best and ruining our lives from the inside out.

What do we need to do to get what rightly belongs to us? We must clean house, uproot, and regraft, *As It Pleases God*, and not what is pleasing to ourselves. How do we start cleaning house, Mentally, Physically, Emotionally, and Spiritually? The initial step is to make a decision. Secondly, *The WHY Blueprint* is designed to *Reverse Engineer* our mindset, helping us make our MARK.

When making a mark or impact, we must allow our goal or mission to become the marksmen. Projecting our goals with a strategy puts the ticketing in our shareability. What is ticketing? It is the exchange part of the HOW-TO process of putting our WHY (What Hurts Us is What Heals Us) to work. Simply put, this is where people buy into what we are doing because there is a connection to our WHO (What Heals Others).

A viable connection is formed when we connect our WHY to the WHO. If we do not know the seeds, roots, and fruits connected to our WHY, it becomes challenging to intertwine or fertilize the WHO. For example, we think cow manure is repulsive, but it is commonly used as a natural fertilizer for crops and gardens. It is rich in nutrients such as nitrogen, phosphorus, and potassium, which are essential for plant growth. We may turn up our noses, but plants and soil welcome cow manure with open arms. In all simplicity, the pain-to-comfort analogy provided a resource and a lifeline for another.

What does our WHY have to do with our seeds, roots, and fruits? A seed is a small object a plant produces that can grow into a new plant. On the other hand, a root is the part of a plant that typically lies below the surface of the soil, anchoring the plant and absorbing water and nutrients. While both are important for the growth and survival of a plant, they serve different functions to produce the fruit, positively or negatively.

However, the goal is to take the average seeds, roots, or fruits to the capital Seeds, Roots, and Fruits. What is the difference? RESPECT. When dealing with all things Spiritual, respect is of great importance, even if we do not understand it or know about it. Yet, our Spirit Man does.

CHAPTER EIGHT
The SEEDED Mindset

Is your mindset dialed in on Greatness? Do you understand what it means to have a mindset of limitlessness? Do you even think you are GREAT? If this book has made it into your hands, you are indeed GREATNESS in seed form. Above all, I believe in you, your seed, and your Predestined Blueprint.

The seeds planted in our minds determine their yield. Even if we think we are not beneficial or unusable, we are salvageable in the Eye of God. For this reason, *The Seeded Mindset* is designed to help paint mental pictures for real-time playback, causing everything to work together for our good, even if it does not look good right now. It does not matter how life appears to the naked eye; there is always a win-win hidden within it, them, or that. Let us go deeper...

Getting back to the WHO (What Heals Others), we must understand how to use our Pollinating Seeds to reach others. What is a Pollinated Seed? Pollination is a crucial process in gardening, affecting the quality and yield of crops.

By transferring pollen from the male part of a plant to the female part, pollination allows for the fertilization of the plant and the production of seeds. It can be done naturally by bees and other insects, or it can be done manually by gardeners. Either way, pollination is essential for successful gardening and a bountiful harvest.

More importantly, fertilization of plants leads to the production of more seeds reproducing after their own kind, creating a cycle of success of its own. The same applies to us, hidden in the Law of Reciprocity. Thus, we have a greater ability to distribute *The WHY Blueprint* embedded in our DNA, while allowing the WHO to gravitate toward our WHY. Here is how the Pollinating Seeds work:

WHAT HEALS OTHERS *is* **WHAT HEALS YOU** *is* **WHAT HUMBLES YOU** *is* **WHAT HONORS YOU**

I am living proof. I have been in the game too long to play around with my seeds, someone else's seeds, or God's precious sheep. Listed below are a few ways to get your Pollinating Seeds distributed, but not limited to such:

- ☐ Set high but realistic goals for yourself and your seeds without settling for defeat or the okey-doke.
- ☐ Pursue your seeded goals with passion, proactiveness, and perseverance, leaving no stone unturned.
- ☐ Seek feedback on your seeds by asking relevant questions.
- ☐ Learn from the mistakes and failures of your seeds.

- ☐ Surround yourself with positive and supportive people.
- ☐ Keep a positive attitude about your seeds, canceling the negative self-talk or mental chatter.
- ☐ Become grateful for everything, including the good, bad, or indifferent.
- ☐ Refrain from fussing, complaining, and fighting.
- ☐ Keep an open mind about new ideas and different perspectives.
- ☐ Take responsibility for your actions, reactions, thoughts, decisions, and seeds.
- ☐ Take time to communicate with your seeds; they will listen, especially when developing a personal relationship with them.
- ☐ Pray for your seeds; we cannot go wrong placing God at the forefront.

What is the purpose of having this list? Seeds are one of the most overlooked commodities known to man. They are usually small and take varying amounts of time to produce results. By the time the seed begins to produce, we have moved on to something else, forgetting what we have sown. Therefore, if it is documented, we have a way of tracking and regrafting our seeds without being blindsided by the Vicissitudes of Life or a cycle of déjà vu.

Seedtime and Harvest will have no mercy on our fruits, especially when they are ignored or disrespected as if they do not exist. With *The Seeded Mindset*, we should be dialed in on this Spiritual Principle. Why? Our seeds, roots, and fruits are connected to us, determining if we are a Tree of Life or a Tree of Death and Destruction.

In *The Why Blueprint*, our character is everything, and if we are not up to par on our character, we may play ourselves short regarding our people skills. When we come into contact with others, we give off the energy of desire, trust, untrustworthiness, caution, question, pity, curiosity, or disgust. Although most will not tell us how they feel, their actions, reactions, and responses will tell us what we need to know without them saying one word. Remember, this works both ways; therefore, when that hellion rises from within, SQUASH IT!

The power of psychology is excellent; however, the powers hidden in our fruits are profound and life-defining! Listen, psychology can work for us on occasion, fool us on occasion, or make a fool out of us on occasion as well, but the Fruits of the Spirit will not! It will grant you the secret instinctual wisdom that trumps any psychological mind game maze!

Most often, we become trained to create mind games and rules on how to get into the minds of others or to determine their character, and we miss out on who we truly are from the inside out. Unfortunately, precious time is wasted playing mind games, primarily when all we need to do is check the fruits. How can something so simple be so profound? According to the Heavenly of Heavens, the moment we think we are ahead of the game by knowing the complexities of manipulation, we become left behind by overlooking the simplicities hidden in plain sight. Frankly, this is like overlooking a dollar to pick up a nickel.

The Seeded Mindset is about uncomplicating people, places, and things by knowing the Divine System. Why? With complications comes stress, anxiety, and duality. Once we become divided as such, our personalities will split, even if we are in denial. Plus, the longer we are in denial, the more splits will occur. How do we recognize a split? Once again, it is identified by our fruits; therefore, it behooves us to focus on mastering the Fruits of the Spirit.

Why must we master the Fruits of the Spirit? It helps the psyche autocorrect by nudging our conscience and connecting to our human senses to alert us. For this reason, we never want to violate the conscience or cause it to lie dormant because our Spiritual Compass guides us toward righteousness or away from imminent danger.

The Fruits of the Spirit can provide profound, life-defining wisdom that psychology cannot match. What is the difference between them? Man created psychology to understand the science of man, and the Fruits of the Spirit are Divinely Created by God to defy science. It is the textbook versus the Bible. So it behooves us to know both sides to establish BALANCE between our faith and reality.

Why must we establish balance Mentally, Physically, Emotionally, and Spiritually? It is easy to get caught up in mind games when trying to understand or manipulate others, but we often miss the true essence of who we are. In so many words, we can become easily brainwashed if we exclude Biblical Knowledge. And if we have all the Biblical Knowledge without living practically and relevantly, we are of no earthly good. What does this mean? We are not relatable or repulsive to be around, lacking authentic people skills. Or, we are hitting people over the head with the Bible instead of living by example in the Spirit of Love.

Checking our seeds, roots, and fruits can save us time and help us focus on what really matters. Above all else, our seeds, roots, and fruits reflect the integrity of our character, which is the foundation of our interactions with others, even if we do not believe they are. However, the numbers or results will not lie to us, even if we lie to ourselves.

When trying to solve a problem, address an issue, or stop lying to ourselves, it is important to get to the seed and root of the matter with an understanding of the fruit, positively or negatively. Using *The Seeded Mindset* helps us identify the underlying cause or source of the problem rather than just addressing the symptoms (fruits). One way to do this is by asking the WHY questions, identifying the problem or issue, and then asking why it is happening. Continue the process until you reach the seeded or rooted cause, then align it with the Word of God and your core values, *As It Pleases Him*.

When Spiritually Aligning ourselves with our core values, we must alleviate the confusion from the inside out, not from the outside in. Why? Approaching Spiritual Alignment from the outside in sends a signal to the Heavenly of Heavens that we are avoiding or deflecting ownership of our role in whatever and with whomever.

WHAT HEALS OTHERS *is* **WHAT HEALS YOU** *is* **WHAT HUMBLES YOU** *is* **WHAT HONORS YOU**

For this reason, *The WHY Blueprint* provides clarification to ensure we can self-correct in the erroring process to avoid having our negative or debauched seeds become roots or fruits. Here are a few core values that God is expecting from us, but not limited to such:

- ☐ Acceptance
- ☐ Accountability
- ☐ Adaptability
- ☐ Authenticity
- ☐ Clarity
- ☐ Compassion
- ☐ Consistency
- ☐ Contentment
- ☐ Courage
- ☐ Creativity
- ☐ Dependability
- ☐ Determination
- ☐ Diligence
- ☐ Discernment
- ☐ Discipline
- ☐ Education
- ☐ Effectiveness
- ☐ Efficiency
- ☐ Empathy
- ☐ Encouragement
- ☐ Endurance
- ☐ Enthusiasm
- ☐ Excellence
- ☐ Faith
- ☐ Flexibility
- ☐ Focus
- ☐ Forgiveness
- ☐ Generosity
- ☐ Gentleness
- ☐ Goodness
- ☐ Grace
- ☐ Gratitude
- ☐ Growth
- ☐ Honesty
- ☐ Humility
- ☐ Imagination

- ☐ Initiative
- ☐ Innovation
- ☐ Integrity
- ☐ Joy
- ☐ Justice
- ☐ Kindness
- ☐ Leadership
- ☐ Learning
- ☐ Love
- ☐ Mercy
- ☐ Modesty
- ☐ Obedience
- ☐ Open-mindedness
- ☐ Optimism
- ☐ Optimism
- ☐ Passion
- ☐ Patience
- ☐ Peace
- ☐ Perseverance
- ☐ Productivity
- ☐ Progress
- ☐ Purity
- ☐ Resilience
- ☐ Resourcefulness
- ☐ Respect
- ☐ Responsibility
- ☐ Sacrifice
- ☐ Self-control
- ☐ Self-improvement
- ☐ Selflessness
- ☐ Self-motivation
- ☐ Service
- ☐ Simplicity
- ☐ Thankfulness
- ☐ Tolerance
- ☐ Trust
- ☐ Understanding
- ☐ Vision
- ☐ Willpower
- ☐ Wisdom
- ☐ Zeal

By embracing these values and striving to live them daily with a work-in-progress mentality, we can honor God and find fulfillment in our lives. The strength and wisdom to live by these core values give us Spiritual Leverage, closing the *Great Divine*.

CHAPTER NINE
Closing the Divide

When closing the *Great Divide*, you must learn and grow with an understanding that *What Hurts You is What Heals You*, primarily if you allow it to do so. If not, your unresolved thoughts, beliefs, traumas, and yokes can become a nightmare from the inside out. Nevertheless, it does not have to remain regardless of what is dividing you right now...there is hope. How? You must master putting on *The Whole Armor of God*, and in this chapter, I will show you how to *Close the Divide* with it.

With *The WHY Blueprint*, we must understand that we are relational beings driven by RELATABILITY. The best way to become relational, *As It Pleases God*, is to understand Spiritual Metaphors and Word Pictures. Why? God is NOT going to speak in a language everyone can understand...He will speak in parables, riddles, puzzles, and so on. Plus, when He sends confirmation about someone, something, or somewhere, we must understand it *Spirit to Spirit*. Thus, we must exercise the MIND to pay attention to all things

Spiritual because it connects to our senses and conscience. If our senses and conscience are keeled, lacking relatability or consistency, our Spiritual Metaphors can become Spiritual Anomalies, which is not ideal in the Eye of God.

One would ask, 'What is a Spiritual Metaphor?' It is a figure of speech comparing two things figuratively or non-literally. Metaphorically, there are Biblical Metaphors throughout the Bible, painting Mental Pictures or conveying a deeper meaning by comparing two seemingly unrelated things. Why do we need metaphors? It gets our mental wheels turning, cleaning out the cobwebs. Most Spiritual Battles occur between our two ears—in the MIND.

We are easily defeated, provoked, ostracized, yoked, or broken if we have a weak mind. On the other hand, if our mind is strong, it becomes our metaphoric power play, especially if we know how to use it, *As It Pleases God.* How so? If our mental playback is good, we become good by default with a bit of tweaking here and there. If the playback is bad, negative, or debauched, we become likewise, getting worse with time.

According to the Heavenly of Heavens, one of the most powerful tools for Spiritual Growth is using Spiritual Metaphors, comparing two things that are not alike but share some common qualities. For example, when we say someone is a 'rising star,' we are not saying they are a star in the sky. It means they have some qualities resembling a star, such as brightness, illumination, or sparkling, helping us create mental pictures to inspire, motivate, or guide us in our Spiritual Journey.

In Ephesians, the Apostle Paul uses a powerful *Spiritual Metaphor* to describe the Spiritual Resources God has given His people. According to Ephesians 6:11, He calls our Spiritual Tools *'The Whole Armor of God,'* giving us the ability to withstand the enemy's wiles.

How can we apply *The Whole Armor of God* to our lives? Here is the deal: The Armor of God is not a literal set of weapons or clothing, but a way of referring to the various aspects of Divine Character Traits needed in Spiritual Battles, ushering in the Supernatural aspects of our being. Plus, it helps us stand firm in our beliefs and resist temptation.

Why do we need *The Whole Armor of God*, especially as Believers? Simply put, *"For we do not wrestle against flesh and blood, but against principalities, against powers, against the rulers of the darkness of this age, against spiritual hosts of wickedness in the heavenly places."* Ephesians 6:12. Most often, we read this scripture, yet we do not fully understand what it entails or its impact on us and those around us. Nor do we understand that we are Spiritual Beings having a human experience. As a result, we walk around like wounded puppies with victim mentalities instead of standing in our rightful place, *As It Pleases God*.

What is our rightful place? In the Eye of God, our rightful place is standing in Divine Authority, *As It Pleases Him*, girding up our loins using the Spiritual Tools He has given us for our Heaven on Earth Experiences. Why is this so important to God? If we cannot stand on our own two feet, we fall down easily, right? So it is in the Realm of the Spirit. When in Spiritual Warfare with ourselves, others, or with God Almighty, we must know what to do and why.

How is it possible to be in Spiritual Warfare with God? When operating in the Spirit of Disobedience, Dullness, Rebellion, Idolatry, Pompousness, and among many other negative character traits, we can become an enemy of God. Blasphemy, right? Wrong! *"Adulterers and adulteresses! Do you not know that friendship with the world is enmity with God? Whoever therefore wants to be a friend of the world makes himself an enemy of God."* James 4:4. Regardless of where we are in life or what we have going on, *"God resist the proud, but gives grace to the humble."* James 4:6.

How is it possible to become an enemy of God, especially when He loves us all? Although He loves us all, He has set forth rules and regulations governing our Kingdom Status. Amid all, it does not exempt us from Spiritual Chastisement, *"For whom the Lord loves He chastens, and scourges every son whom He receives."* Hebrews 12:6. What does all of this mean? Not only does God correct us, but He will also test us or allow the enemy to train us through debauched acts; therefore, it behooves us to put on *The Whole Armor of God*.

How can we use God's Armor against Him? We do not use it against Him; He created them for us and through us. In all clarity, first and foremost, we use our Spiritual Armor to protect us from ourselves. Secondly, we use it to prevent the enemy from turning us against ourselves with seeds of doubt, fear, anger, jealousy, envy, pride, greed, coveting, and competitiveness.

Regardless of whether we are enemies of God or ourselves, we have the capacity to overcome anything with anyone. What about becoming an enemy to others? We cannot become an enemy of another without becoming an enemy of ourselves first. All else is an illusion that we have control over; therefore, we have the power to change our MINDSET for the greater good by putting on *The Whole Armor of God*.

Above all, we never want to become enemies of God or ourselves. If we do, we can attach ourselves to the negative aspects of the human psyche, contending with the next man. What does this mean? We will think we are better than the next person, belittling those appearing beneath us to satiate the psyche. While at the same time, not realizing this is happening as we plot our downfall of shame.

As we all know, there is good and bad in everyone that must be contained, *As It Pleases God*. Our good should ALWAYS outweigh the bad, period! What if our bad outweighs the good? Repent, forgive, usher in the Holy Trinity, and put on *The Whole Armor of God*.

What is the significance of each piece of *The Whole Armor of God*? Paul lists six pieces of Spiritual Armor:

1. Belt of Truth
2. Breastplate of Righteousness
3. Shoes of the Gospel of Peace
4. Shield of Faith
5. Helmet of Salvation
6. Sword of The Spirit

We can tiptoe around *The Whole Armor of God or* put it on. Regardless of our choice, we have a right to them at any given moment, and no one is exempt from having this opportunity. For this reason, let us learn about them, building value in the Spiritual Tools designed to save our lives and Bloodline, restoring us to our own.

When putting on the *Whole Armor of God*, what is He expecting from us? He does not want us to become careless with our Spiritual Armor. Here is what He is expecting from us, but not limited to such:

- ☐ **Wisdom**: The ability to think critically, learn from experience, and apply knowledge to different situations.

- ☐ **Courage**: The willingness to face fear, danger, or difficulty with confidence and determination.

- ☐ **Justice**: The sense of fairness, equality, and respect for the rights and dignity of others.

- ☐ **Temperance**: The moderation of one's desires, impulses, and emotions.

- ☐ **Prudence**: Practicing good judgment, caution, and foresight in practical matters.

- ☐ **Fortitude**: The strength of the Mind, Body, Soul, and Spirit to endure hardship, pain, or adversity.

- ☐ **Charity**: The generosity and kindness towards others, especially those in need or downtrodden.

- ☐ **Faith**: The trust and belief in God, oneself, and others.
- ☐ **Hope**: The positive expectation set forth with confidence in the future, despite challenges or uncertainties.

- ☐ **Love**: The deep affection and attachment to someone or something, and the willingness to sacrifice for their good.

Can we live up to these standards? Absolutely. Keep reading, and I will show you how.

The Belt of Truth

As we put on the *Whole Armor of God*, the first section of the armor is the *Belt of Truth*. In ancient times, a belt was not only a decorative accessory but also a practical one. It held together the loose garments of a soldier and provided a place to attach other pieces of equipment, such as a sword or a dagger. This BELT symbolizes READINESS and PREPAREDNESS for action.

Are you ready? Are you prepared? Most would ask, 'For what?' My answer would be, 'For anything!' When suiting up with the *Whole Armor of God*, we must stay on ready.

The *Belt of Truth* will uphold us in the Spirit of Truth, helping us discern the truth from falsehood. If we gird up our loins with falsehood, it has the propensity to break our backs in due time. Whereas truthfulness builds our integral backbone, helping us STAND for the Kingdom of God with enlightenment, wisdom, and inner guidance.

Once we become Spiritual Elites, *As It Pleases God*, we are ushered into the Divine Elements of the Kingdom. What does this mean in layman's terms? It is the act of going from a lower level or case letter to a higher level or case letter of RESPECT with Divine Enlightenment, Wisdom, Guidance, and Secrets. However, one cannot glean from this Spiritual Reservoir, or they will have LIMITS unless they become trained to do so. Why? Due to our human nature of abuse, misuse, or misunderstanding.

Suppose one goes to the dark side to gain limited access to the Divine Elements that we are not privy to handle. In this case, the Spiritual Violations will appear within the human psyche with a combative yo-yo effect. What does this mean? They are all over the place with their character, going from hot to cold with little or no self-control. In addition, they will also spread rotten fruits and disrespectful toxicity with a belt of lies, breaking themselves and others down. By trying to beat the System of God, we inadvertently bring this belt back to our own house with the lust of the eyes, the lusts of the flesh, and the pride of life.

What makes one person better than the next one, especially when dealing with Divine Elements? No one is better than anyone...this is why God requires humility and adhering to Spiritual Principles. Those operating at an Elite Spiritual Level, *As It Pleases God*, operate in an authentic guise of humility, going undetected by most, but can positively IMPACT all they encounter. More importantly, they possess EXCELLENT people skills to feed God's sheep. Even if someone tries to taint their reputation with lies, debauchery, and dismay, or goes out of their way to find fault in them, they will come forth as pure gold without shame.

Why are they not brought to shame? If God uses them, according to their Predestined Blueprint, everything will work together for their good, regardless of how it appears to the naked eye. Furthermore, when using the Fruits of the Spirit, *As It Pleases God*, they are designed to expose or repose, letting them know who is who with the Divine Elements of the Kingdom. What do expose and repose have to do with anything? Our Spiritual Fruits will expose who we are, or they will calm the psyche down.

Why must we become trained to partake of the Divine Elements of the Kingdom? A Spiritual Foundation, *As It Pleases God*, requires the right character, fruits, behaviors, and purification to avoid creating generational curses or prevent our Divine Compass from rusting. In Spirituality, we either use it the right or wrong way...there is no in-between; however, there is always a Rod of Correction or Pruning Tool.

Whether we are on the correcting, pruning, gleaning, or tilling side of life, we have options. What are they?

- ☐ We have the Word of God.
- ☐ We have the covering of the Blood of Jesus.
- ☐ We have the guidance of the Holy Spirit.

- ☐ We have daily repentance.
- ☐ We can continually forgive.
- ☐ We can become a work-in-progress.
- ☐ We can Spiritually Till our own ground.
- ☐ We can use the Fruits of the Spirit.
- ☐ We have the Spiritual Right to God's Divine Grace and Mercy.
- ☐ We can tap into our Predestined Blueprint.

These are extremely important to avoid operating in Spiritual Error or Omission. Why is this list of options so important? It lets our conscience kick in to alert, protect, or send red flags, letting us know whether our Belt of Truth is loose or unbuckled, allowing us to self-correct, self-protect, or exhibit self-control.

According to the Heavenly of Heavens, it only takes a fraction of a second to blur the lines of truth or come back into alignment, yet we must know the difference and proceed accordingly. Our commitment to honesty, integrity, and acceptance of God's Divine Word is the ultimate source of truth, correction, and protection that will guard us against deception and falsehood. Therefore, *"Sanctify them by Your Truth. Your word is truth."* John 17:17.

The Breastplate of Righteousness

Once our *Belt of Truth* is firmly secure, we can put on the second piece of the armor, the *Breastplate of Righteousness*. With this breastplate, can you commit to doing the right thing when things go wrong? Can you become the best version of yourself doing what you were called to do? Are you willing to protect your heart? Are you willing to purify your heart of all its impurities? Are you committed to living a life pleasing to God?

The *Breastplate of Righteousness* refers explicitly to the piece of armor that protects the chest, heart, and other vital organs, representing a life of moral purity, positioning, identity, righteousness, and integrity in Christ Jesus. All of these protect the Spiritual Organs needed for our Kingdomly Duties, shielding us from the accusations and condemnation of our internal and external enemies. It also frees us from guilt, shame, or unworthiness by those seeking to pollute, corrupt, or distract us from doing what we were called to do.

For the record, the *Breastplate of Righteousness* is not the same as self-righteousness. What is the difference between them? The trap of self-righteousness leads us into a form of pride and hypocrisy, invoking jealousy, envy, pride, greed, coveting, and competitiveness. In contrast, *The Breastplate of Righteousness* is a gift of grace and mercy from God Almighty, not something we earn by our works or efforts. All we need to do is put it on, *As It Pleases Him,* with a work-in-progress mentality.

What if we opt not to use the work-in-progress mentality, *As It Pleases God*? Then, we will please ourselves by default. Unfortunately, the enemy will use our underlying self-righteousness to weaken our self-made breastplate, causing their darts to penetrate.

According to the Heavenly of Heavens, using *The Breastplate of Righteousness* will cause the enemy's darts to ricochet off us. So here is the deal: When dealing with *The WHY Blueprint*, we have two options:

1. Penetrate.
2. Ricochet.

Positive and negative penetrations of the Mind, Body, Soul, and Spirit are real. Unfortunately, this is how we get soul ties, yokes, and bondages, and if we DO NOT put on *The Whole Armor of God*, we become susceptible to the enemy's wiles, even if we pretend to be Holy Ghost-Filled and Fire Baptized. On the other hand, to cause soul ties, yokes, and bondages to ricochet off our Spiritual Breastplate, we must do a few things, but not limited to such:

- ☐ Place God first, developing a *Spirit to Spirit* Relationship.
- ☐ Cover ourselves with the Blood of Jesus.
- ☐ Awaken the Holy Spirit to become ONE with our Spirit.
- ☐ Repent, forgive, and give thanks.
- ☐ Document instructions.
- ☐ Come into a Divine Agreement for the UNVEILING of our Divine Blueprint.
- ☐ Counteract negatives into positives, creating a win-win.
- ☐ Share information, thoughts, or whatever for the greater good.

Do we have a say in whether a dart penetrates or ricochets? Of course, especially when we are in Purpose on purpose! Let me give you ONE UP for the Kingdom...God will protect the VISION belonging to Him, which is our reason for being. If one does not know what it is or is not, it is time to get in the know.

Here is what we must glean before going any further: *"Put away the gods that your fathers served beyond the River and in Egypt, and serve the Lord. And if it is evil in your eyes to serve the Lord, choose this day whom you will serve, whether the gods your fathers served in the region beyond the River, or the gods of the Amorites in whose land you dwell. But as for me and my house, we will serve the Lord."* Joshua 24:14-15.

Why is choosing so important when using *The Breastplate of Righteousness*? Self-righteousness is a counterfeit version of Spiritual Righteousness, relying on our own standards, idiosyncrasies, and opinions. In addition, it causes us to judge others harshly and look down on them while ignoring our faults and sins.

Unfortunately, judgmental behavior causes us to think we are better than others and deserve God's favor more than they do. As a result, it puts a damper or Spiritual Block on our Predestined Blueprint. More importantly, if we do not know what it is or are living OUT of PURPOSE, we have no reason to judge another man's journey, especially if we are not lending a helping hand.

Are we really living OUT of Purpose on purpose? Absolutely! When we trust in our own knowledge, understanding, accomplishments, and strength, rather than God's grace, mercy, and power, or giving thanks, it creates a hiccup in our Spiritual System.

When dealing with self-righteousness, it is difficult to examine yourself without having an outside source as a reflection; therefore, here are a few mirroring questions to ask yourself, but not limited to such:

- ☐ Do you avoid repenting?
- ☐ Do you refuse to forgive?
- ☐ Do you hate apologizing?
- ☐ Do you avoid saying, 'Please or Thank You'?
- ☐ Do you resist correction?

- ☐ Do you despise someone giving you instructions?
- ☐ Do you alienate people who cannot benefit you?
- ☐ Do you always take without giving back?

Why should we query ourselves often? Self-righteousness is a form of idolatry. Exalting ourselves above God is a quick way to bring shame to our names or Bloodline.

When dealing with self-righteousness, we will all experience this learning curve as a part of our Spiritual Classroom; therefore, we cannot be hard on ourselves. Simply learn, understand, grow, and sow back into the Kingdom of God when called upon. What if we aced the above questions? Congratulations! Let us go deeper, stirring the pot a little more.

Self-righteousness will present itself in various ways, thinning our Spiritual Armor. Listed below are a few ways thinning occurs, but not limited to such:

- ☐ An unwillingness to admit fault, own our truth, or take responsibility for mistakes.
- ☐ There is a tendency to judge, demean, and criticize others while ignoring one's own flaws.
- ☐ There is a belief that one's worldview, beliefs, or values are the only correct ones.
- ☐ There is a need to be seen as morally superior to others.
- ☐ There is a tendency to be overly critical, dismissive, or judgmental of those who do not share one's beliefs.
- ☐ A refusal to consider alternative viewpoints or opinions.
- ☐ An inability to empathize with others or see things from their perspective.

- ☐ There is a tendency to be defensive or argumentative when challenged.
- ☐ There is an unwillingness to compromise or find common ground with others.
- ☐ There is a tendency to use shame, cussing, yelling, or guilt to control others.
- ☐ There is a belief that one is always right and others are always wrong.
- ☐ There is a tendency to be dogmatic or inflexible.
- ☐ There is a tendency to use harsh or judgmental language when speaking about others.
- ☐ There is a belief that one is better than others because of one's race, gender, or social status.
- ☐ There is a tendency to be smug, taking credit for the work of others without acknowledging them or giving thanks.
- ☐ There is a lack of humility or willingness to learn from others.
- ☐ There is a belief that one's own opinions or beliefs are more important than others' feelings or experiences.

Why must we know about self-righteousness along with *The Breastplate of Righteousness*? It protects the believer's heart from the accusations and temptations of the enemy, who is the accuser of the brethren. By doing a self-filtering on ourselves, we can trip the enemy up instead of being tripped by the lack of knowledge when accused. Is this Biblical? Of course. "*Then I heard a loud voice saying in heaven, 'Now salvation, and strength, and the kingdom of our God, and the power of His Christ have come, for the accuser of our brethren, who accused them before our God day and night, has been cast down.'*" Revelation 12:10.

Why would someone accuse us? Unbeknown to most, self-righteousness exposes the heart and its weaknesses to the enemy; therefore, when accused, we get out of character easily, showing our true colors and real fruits. Remember, what is in us will come out, especially when under pressure.

In dealing with *The Breastplate of Righteousness*, accusations are a part of the process, letting us know: *"They overcame him by the blood of the Lamb and by the word of their testimony."* Revelation 12:11. We can do likewise by knowing our strengths, traumas, and weaknesses and working on them consistently, *As It Pleases God*. What can this do for us? It de-weaponizes the enemy, giving us Spiritual Leverage as opposed to someone who does not know anything about themselves or lives in denial, lies, or debauchery. We must know this beyond a shadow of a doubt; if not, we can 'get got' by the enemy's tricks, words, and behaviors designed to zap our peace. The bottom line is that when it is all said and done, *The Breastplate of Righteousness* is always hidden in our STORY.

The Shoes of the Gospel of Peace

Now that we have the *Belt of Truth* and *Breastplate of Righteousness* firmly secured, we can put on the third piece of the armor, the *Shoes of the Gospel of Peace*. In the Spiritual Realm, the *Shoes of Peace* represent our relationship with God through Christ Jesus.

When putting on your shoes, have you ever wished you could walk confidently and peacefully without fear or anxiety? If so, you are not alone. Many struggle with finding peace in their relationships, whether with God, themselves, family, friends, coworkers, or even strangers.

But what if I told you there is a way to walk peacefully, no matter what the situation is or who you are dealing with? What if I told you that the secret to peace is not changing others but yourself? And what if I told you that the key to changing yourself is in your shoes? Yes, you read it right. Your shoes. Or, more specifically, your *Shoes of the Gospel of Peace* assist you in walking in the Spirit of Excellence, *As It Pleases God*.

In a world of conflict and strife, *The Shoes of Peace* enable us to walk according to God's Divine Will, Guidance, and Direction, becoming peacemakers. They also enable us to stand firm in our faith and resist the enemy's attacks. Let us go deeper...

The *Shoes of the Gospel of Peace* are a metaphor for the ATTITUDE and MINDSET you need to walk in peace, *As It Pleases God*, instead of pleasing yourself. Putting on *The Whole Armor* takes a little precision to finetune the adornment of our Spiritual Armor, helping us navigate difficult situations with grace, resilience, and know-how. While simultaneously positioning ourselves to allow the HOW-TO to track us down.

Why would the HOW-TO track us? *"For we walk by faith, not by sight."* 2 Corinthians 5:7. For this reason, we must activate our Spiritual Compass to energize our shoes, be it naturally or Supernaturally. How do we make this make sense? Simply put, we must know when to stay on our feet and when to shake the dust off.

For example, wherever we place our feet, if there is NO PEACE in our Good News, we must keep it moving in the Spirit of Excellence. Please allow me to Spiritually Align: *"And whoever will not receive you nor hear your words, when you depart from that house or city, shake off the dust from your feet."* Matthew 10:14.

What if we are running away from our issues? If we are running from issues, it indicates that we are not operating with the *Shoes of the Gospel of Peace*, so shaking the dust off our feet is NOT APPLICABLE here. Why would this not apply to everyone? We must first have the *Shoes of Peace*, be on a Spiritual Assignment, in a Spiritual Classroom, or operate in our Blueprinted Purpose. With all due respect, shaking the dust off CANNOT be an excuse for NOT doing what is required of us.

Furthermore, suppose we are in a chaotic state of being or in a chaotic situation. In this case, we contribute to our condition somehow, even if we are a victim, in denial, or caught in a cycle of déjà vu. Thus, we must check our fruits, seeds, roots, character, behaviors, spoken words, inner chatter, and mindset.

The Gospel of Peace is the GOOD NEWS that God loves us, forgives us, and reconciles us to himself and to each other through Jesus Christ. If we dare to put it on daily, like we put our shoes, it will grant us peace with God, peace within ourselves, and peace with others.

How is it humanly possible to put on peace, especially when it is an intangible commodity? First, the *Shoes of the Gospel of Peace* represent the readiness to share and live in harmony with God, ourselves, and others. Secondly, according to Galatians 5:22-23, the Fruits of The Spirit are the characterizable qualities the Holy Spirit produces in us as we use them and abide in Christ. Thirdly, when putting on the *Shoes of the Gospel of Peace* with Love, Joy, Peace, Patience, Kindness, Goodness, Faithfulness, Gentleness, and Self-Control, it will change the trajectory of our lives positively, enabling us to represent the Good News by default.

Spiritual Fruits are evidence of your Spiritual Growth and the source of Divine Inspiration. Wearing the *Shoes of the Gospel of Peace* with the Fruits of The Spirit allows us to walk in harmony without feeling like we are walking on eggshells, trying to avoid conflict, judgment, or criticism from others.

How do we metaphorically put on the *Shoes of the Gospel of Peace* in our daily interactions? Here are some practical steps that can help you walk in peace, but not limited to such:

- ☐ You must recognize your need for peace.
- ☐ You must admit when you are not at peace and need God's help to find it.
- ☐ You must become aware of when you feel stressed, angry, hurt, bitter, fearful, or insecure to counteract them positively.
- ☐ When facing challenges, conflicts, or pressures, you must pinpoint when you are overwhelmed to avoid imploding or exploding.
- ☐ You must recognize when you are tempted to blame others, lash out, or withdraw. Doing so helps you redirect your authority and responsibility.
- ☐ You must be willing to receive God's peace by faith.
- ☐ You must understand God's peace is NOT something you can earn, buy, deserve, or achieve by your own efforts. It is a GIFT that He gives freely to those who believe and trust in Him, using the Fruits of the Spirit.
- ☐ You must know God's peace is not dependent on your circumstances but on His Divine Promises.
- ☐ You must understand God's peace is not a feeling but a state of being.
- ☐ You must release your worries, doubts, or fears; they are the biggest enemies of peace.
- ☐ You must avoid focusing too much on the problems while working on the solutions wholeheartedly.

☐ You must avoid focusing on the what-ifs and pay attention to the what-is of your reality.

What if our practical steps toward peace do not work for us? Suppose we find ourselves in a situation where our efforts to achieve peace are ineffective. In this case, we may need to reflect on our approach and try to identify the seed, root, or underlying cause. Sometimes, it might be beneficial to involve a third party, such as a mediator or a counselor, who can help us understand the situation better and guide us through the process. We should always be open-minded, flexible, and ready to adapt our approach.

Additionally, we should never give up on our pursuit of peace and continue striving to find resolutions. If it is beyond our capacity, do not worry about it, pray, repent, forgive, and keep it moving in the Spirit of Excellence.

Wearing the *Shoes of the Gospel of Peace* helps us to walk in love and grace. Romans 10:15 says, *"How beautiful are the feet of those who bring good news!"* The Gospel of Peace is not only something we believe, but something we share. As we wear the *Shoes of the Gospel of Peace*, we are ready to go wherever God sends us and to proclaim his love and grace to everyone we meet.

What do the *Shoes of the Gospel of Peace* look like in the Eye of God? At a glance, when we are on Spiritual Assignment, *As It Pleases Him*, we are NOT judgmental, harsh, or hostile, but gentle, kind, and compassionate. We are NOT selfish, greedy, or proud, but generous, humble, and servant-hearted. We are peacemakers, reconcilers, and forgivers, NOT divisive, quarrelsome, or bitter.

Wearing the *Shoes of the Gospel of Peace* helps us to run the race of life with endurance and joy. Hebrews 12:1-2 says,

"Therefore, since we are surrounded by such a great cloud of witnesses, let us throw off everything that hinders and the sin that so easily entangles. And let us run with perseverance the race marked out for us, fixing our eyes on Jesus, the pioneer and perfecter of faith. For the joy set before him he endured the cross, scorning its shame, and sat down at the right hand of the throne of God." More importantly, this is not only something we share but something we live.

As we wear the *Shoes of the Gospel of Peace*, we are required to live by example, not weighed down by guilt, shame, or fear, but freed by grace, forgiveness, and hope. We are not distracted by worldly pleasures, pressures, or problems, but focused on our Heavenly Treasures, Divine Purposes, and Promises, *As It Pleases God*. Is it possible to maintain this state of being or mindset consistently? Of course! The KEY is to know what to do, when to do, how to do, why to do, where to do, and with whom. When you are alone, dealing with yourself, listed below are a few tips on maintaining, but not limited to such:

- ☐ Take deep breaths and focus on the present moment.
- ☐ Practice gratitude for what you have in your life.
- ☐ Engage in happenings, activities, or events that bring joy, peace, and relaxation.
- ☐ Spend time in nature and appreciate its beauty.
- ☐ Connect with loved ones and build meaningful relationships.
- ☐ Practice forgiveness and let go of grudges.
- ☐ Cultivate compassion for yourself and others.
- ☐ Set boundaries and prioritize self-care.
- ☐ Engage in mindful practices like meditation.
- ☐ Seek out professional help if needed to address mental health concerns.

- ☐ Focus on what you can control and let go of what you cannot.
- ☐ Avoid negative self-talk or mental chatter, replacing it with positive affirmations, words, quotes, or pictures.
- ☐ Practice active listening and communicate effectively with others.
- ☐ Cultivate a sense of purpose and meaning in your life.
- ☐ Embrace change and see it as an opportunity for growth.
- ☐ Practice resilience and bounce back from setbacks.
- ☐ Show kindness to yourself and others.
- ☐ Take time to reflect and learn from past experiences.
- ☐ Practice acceptance and embrace your imperfections.
- ☐ Find ways to serve others and give back.

Wearing the *Shoes of the Gospel of Peace* is non-negotiable for us to maintain our Spiritual Stance. They equip us to stand firmly in our beliefs, exhibit empathy and kindness, and persist through life's hurdles with determination and contentment. Therefore, let us make it a habit to wear the *Shoes of the Gospel of Peace* daily and relish their benefits.

The Shield of Faith

After adorning ourselves with the *Belt of Truth*, *Breastplate of Righteousness*, and *Shoes of the Gospel of Peace*, we can pick up the fourth piece of our Spiritual Armor, the *Shield of Faith*.

Many people struggle with their faith at some point in their lives. They may doubt the existence of our Heavenly Father, the validity of the Word of God, or the relevance of the Church. They may feel distant from God, disappointed by His actions, or discouraged by their circumstances. Then again, they may wonder if faith is worth it, whether it makes a difference, or if it is even possible.

Do people really question their faith? Absolutely! Unfortunately, this is happening from the pews to the pulpit...it is just hidden under layers of something else. For this reason, I make it my business to answer the tough questions, helping us to understand all things Spiritual.

The *Shield of Faith* is a vital piece of Spiritual Armor a Believer can wear. Why? It protects us against the enemy's fiery darts and the doubts and fears disrupting our daily walk. The Shield of Faith is not something we can create, manufacture, buy, or sell. It is an intangible, developed GIFT from God, connecting us back to Him, our Divine Blueprint, and Spirituality.

The Bible says, "*Now faith is the substance of things hoped for, the evidence of things not seen.*" Hebrews 11:1. Faith is not based on our feelings, circumstances, or events, but on God's Divine Word, Power, Covenants, and Promises, resulting in the manifestation of whatever or whomever. What does this mean? Faith is our manifesting or shielding power connecting the unseen to the seen, and the seen to the unseen.

Our Shield of Faith is NOT a one-and-done occurrence. It is a developed relationship between our faith, hope, and love, molding factors or bonding agents. Really? Yes, really! Please allow me to Spiritually Align, "*And now abide faith, hope, love, these three; but the greatest of these is love.*" 1 Corinthians 13:13. If someone proclaims they have Supernatural Faith, and I do not see their capacity to love...I do not believe them. Why? Natural faith, such as eating, drinking, moving, sitting, standing, driving, and so on, does not require the capacity to love God, ourselves, and others. Frankly, God has given us a ONE-UP with no strings attached to our natural faith.

On the other hand, with Supernatural Faith, love is a prerequisite. Why is love a requirement, especially when we have free will to love whomever, whatever, and whenever? Of course, we have free will to love how we choose and with whom. Nevertheless, when tapping into Spirituality, we play by God's Rules, not ours.

The Spiritual Rules and Principles of our Kingdomly Capacity are hidden in our capacity to love, *As It Pleases God*. If we do not know this, it is a possibility that we may be operating in Spiritual Error or Omission. Blasphemy, right? Wrong. "*Love suffers long and is kind; love does not envy; love does not parade itself, is not puffed up; does not behave rudely, does not seek its own, is not provoked, thinks no evil; does not rejoice in iniquity, but rejoices in the truth; bears all things, believes all things, hopes all things, endures all things. Love never fails.*" 1 Corinthians 13:4-8. The lack of love does not make us bad or evil; it simply limits us to a certain level or capacity.

What is the purpose of God limiting us, especially when we are Believers? If we can do evil or bad things with little faith, how much damage can we do with Supernatural Faith and Power? That is precisely my point! For this reason, God has placed limits on our Spiritual Capacity, especially if we are evil, rude, negative, or hateful. Now, if we go to the dark side, we can gain a little more power or back door insight with a simulation of faith, but there is a HIGH price to pay for the Spiritual Violations. What is the cost? It will vary from person to person, situation to situation, bias to bias, trauma to trauma, culture to culture, and so on.

Regardless of our level of faith or the lack thereof, I would not suggest that we play around with Spiritual Matters we do not understand. Why? It will cause the pit within the human psyche to become deeper and deeper until we become totally lost from the inside out with dissatisfaction, ungratefulness, and unpleasantness, making us putrefied. Operating in folly as such inadvertently diminishes our faith, opting to control everything and everyone, including God. For this reason, wisdom and folly will do a number on the psyche. Is this Biblical? I would have it no other way, *"Dead flies putrefy the perfumer's ointment, and cause it to give off a foul odor; So, does a little folly to one respected for wisdom and honor. A wise man's heart is at his right hand, but a fool's heart at his left."* Ecclesiastes 10:1-2.

Our faith will follow suit when we are divided due to fear, doubt, or insecurity. What is the purpose of becoming divided for the lack of faith? We should not become divided, but lingering fear, doubt, and insecurity will have their way, especially if we do not know what to do about it, them, or that. Here is what we must know: *"But let him ask in faith, with no doubting, for he who doubts is like a wave of the sea driven and tossed by the wind. For let not that man suppose that he will receive anything from the Lord; he is a double-minded man, unstable in all his ways."* James 1:6-8.

How can we counteract having a double mind? According to James 1:5, *"If any of you lacks wisdom, let him ask of God, who gives to all liberally and without reproach, and it will be given to him."* We will all go through the testing of our faith to develop wisdom and patience. Without being tested, we will not know where we stand with our faith. Please allow me to Spiritually Align: *"My brethren, count it all joy when you fall into various trials, knowing that the testing of your faith produces patience.*

But let patience have its perfect work, that you may be perfect and complete, lacking nothing." James 1:2-4.

How do we grow and exercise our faith? First, we must get into the Word of God and quote the scriptures relating to our wants, needs, desires, or issues back to Him. Why? *"Faith comes by hearing, and hearing by the word of God."* Romans 10:17. God's Unchanging Word reveals His Divine Will, Ways, Promises, Character, Plans, and Works.

Secondly, obedience enables us to become Spiritually Usable in or out of the Kingdom, feeding His sheep. Obedience in faith is not merely a set of rules to be followed but a way of life rooted in a deep relationship with God, *Spirit to Spirit.* How? It involves listening to God's voice and responding with a heart surrendered to His Divine Will, doing what we were called to do. James 1:22 says, *"But be doers of the word, and not hearers only, deceiving yourselves."* So, you are sadly mistaken if you think you can sit on your hands, doing nothing for the Kingdom of God!

Thirdly, we need to take action! We must put our faith to work; if not, it lays dormant. *"What does it profit, my brethren, if someone says he has faith but does not have works? Can faith save him? If a brother or sister is naked and destitute of daily food, and one of you says to them, "Depart in peace, be warmed and filled," but you do not give them the things which are needed for the body, what does it profit? Thus also faith by itself, if it does not have works, is dead. But someone will say, "You have faith, and I have works." Show me your faith without your works, and I will show you my faith by my works. You believe that there is one God. You do well. Even the demons believe—and tremble! But do you want to know, O foolish man, that faith without works is dead? Was not Abraham our father justified by works when he offered Isaac his son on the altar? Do you see that faith was working together with his works, and by works faith was made perfect? And the Scripture* was fulfilled which says, "Abraham believed God, and it was accounted to him for righteousness." And he was called the friend of God. You see then that a man is justified by works, and not by faith only. Likewise, was not Rahab the harlot also justified by works when she received the messengers and sent them out another way? For as the body without the spirit is dead, so faith without works is dead also." James 2:14-26.

Fourthly, we need to share our faith. "But sanctify the Lord God in your hearts, and always be ready to give a defense to everyone who asks you a reason for the hope that is in you, with meekness and fear." 1 Peter 3:15. Sharing our faith is not only a way to bless others, but also a way to strengthen our own faith and to glorify God through the Power of our Testimony.

The *Shield of Faith* is not something that we can take for granted or neglect. Listed below are a few examples of what the Shield of Faith can do for us, but not limited to such:

- ☐ Provides comfort in times of uncertainty and stress.
- ☐ Increases hope and optimism for the future.
- ☐ Promotes a sense of purpose and meaning in life.
- ☐ Helps to develop positive values and morals.
- ☐ Encourages forgiveness and compassion towards others.
- ☐ Provides a sense of community and belonging.
- ☐ Helps to cope with loss and grief.
- ☐ Promotes resilience and the ability to bounce back from adversity.
- ☐ Enhances personal growth and self-awareness.
- ☐ Encourages mindfulness and living in the present moment.
- ☐ Promotes inner peace and calmness.
- ☐ Helps to reduce anxiety and depression.
- ☐ Enhances relationships with others and promotes empathy.

- ☐ Provides a sense of accountability and responsibility for one's actions.
- ☐ Encourages gratitude and appreciation for all things, experiences, and people.
- ☐ Promotes a healthier lifestyle through well-being consciousness.
- ☐ Helps to overcome addiction and destructive behaviors.
- ☐ Provides a sense of direction and guidance in life.
- ☐ Encourages unselfishness, sharing, and giving back to the Divine Reservoir of Greatness.
- ☐ Promotes a sense of connection with something or someone greater than oneself using our people skills.

Building Faith may not be easy, and the hidden struggles of faith are real. But it is doable with the Holy Trinity and the Fruits of the Spirit at the forefront, knowing what to do and why we are doing it. According to the Heavenly of Heavens, it bridges the gap in walking by faith with our eyes wide open or with them sealed shut. What does this mean? It is easier to walk by faith, not sight, primarily when our Spiritual Eyes, Ears, and Mouth are Kingdomly Cued instead of doing it blind, deaf, mute, and stiff-necked.

How do we avoid becoming blind, deaf, mute, and stiff-necked? Accept the Holy Trinity, repent, forgive, use the Fruits of the Spirit, and behave Christlike. Then, the Holy Spirit will begin to remove the scales from our eyes, open our ears to hear the Voice of God, and grant Kingdom Utterances through a Spiritual Classroom, equipping, training, and testing us with Spiritual Tools one by one. Remember, this is not an overnight process; development, *As It Pleases God*, takes time, but having *The WHY Blueprint* cuts down on the trial and error process.

Our Shield of Faith is a powerful Spiritual Tool that allows us to overcome challenges, cope with stress, and achieve our goals. Yet, the question is, 'How do we build faith in God and ourselves? Here are a few ways to strengthen your faith and live a more fulfilling life, but not limited to such:

- ☐ Pray or meditate daily. Prayer, fasting, and meditation connect us with Divine Wisdom and Guidance. They can also calm the Mind, Body, Soul, and Spirit, reducing anxiety and increasing gratitude.

- ☐ Read inspirational books, the Word of God, or applicable scriptures. Reading uplifting words can inspire, motivate, and remind us of the truths we believe in. They can also provide us with practical advice and examples of how to apply our faith in everyday situations.

- ☐ Join a faith community of Believers. Being part of a group of people who share our beliefs and values can support, encourage, and challenge us to grow. We can also learn from each other, serve, and celebrate together.

- ☐ Engage in Servanthood. Serving others is one of the best ways to express our faith and show our love. It can also help us develop compassion, empathy, and generosity. We can serve others by volunteering, donating, or simply being kind and helpful.

- ☐ Practice gratitude. Gratitude is acknowledging and appreciating the good, bad, or indifferent things in our lives. We can practice gratitude by keeping a journal, saying thank you, or expressing it in prayer or meditation.

- ☐ Listen to uplifting music or podcasts. Music and podcasts can influence our mood, energy, and thoughts. Listening to positive and uplifting ones can boost our faith, inspire us, and make us feel happy. We can also sing along, dance, or share them with others.

- ☐ Watch inspiring movies or shows. Movies and shows can also affect our emotions, perspectives, and actions. Watching inspiring and faith-based ones can strengthen our faith, teach us lessons, and entertain us. We can also discuss them with others or reflect on them in writing.

- ☐ Write affirmations or declarations. Affirmations and declarations are positive statements we say or write to affirm our faith and declare our intentions. They can also help us reprogram our subconscious mind, overcome limiting beliefs, and manifest our desires. We can write them on cards, posters, or sticky notes and place them where we can see them often. Or, we can document them in *The WHY Blueprint* Journal.

- ☐ Visualize your goals or dreams. Visualization is imagining our goals or dreams as if they have already been achieved. It can also help us activate our faith, attract opportunities, and take action. We can visualize by closing our eyes, using pictures, or creating a vision board.

- ☐ Testify or share your faith with others. Testifying or sharing our faith with others is a way of expressing our gratitude, spreading our message, and inspiring others. It can also help us reinforce our beliefs, overcome doubts, and connect with like-minded people. We can testify or share our faith by speaking, writing, or posting on social media.

- ☐ Seek guidance or counsel from mentors or leaders. Guidance or counsel from mentors or leaders is a valuable resource that can help us grow in our faith and overcome challenges. They can also provide us with wisdom, feedback, and support. We can seek guidance or counsel from pastors, teachers, coaches, or friends with more experience or knowledge than we have.

- ☐ Attend workshops or seminars on faith topics. Workshops or seminars on faith topics are educational events that can help us learn new skills, insights, or strategies to enhance our faith and live better lives. They can also expose us to different perspectives, experiences, and resources. We can attend workshops or seminars online or in person.

- ☐ Take courses or classes on faith subjects. Courses or classes on faith subjects are more formal and structured ways of learning about our faith and related topics. They can also help us deepen our understanding, improve our skills, and earn credentials or certificates. We can take courses or classes online or in person.

- ☐ Read blogs or articles on faith issues. Blogs or articles on faith issues are short and easy-to-read sources of information and inspiration that can help us stay updated on current trends, events, or debates related to our faith and its implications for society. They can also provide us with tips, stories, or opinions we can relate to or learn from.

- ☐ Study the lives of faithful people. Studying the lives of faithful people can inspire us, motivate us, and teach us how to apply our faith in different situations. We can learn from their successes, failures, struggles, and victories. We can study the lives of faithful people by reading biographies, watching documentaries, or listening to podcasts.

- ☐ Memorize or recite verses or quotes. Memorizing or reciting verses or quotes can help us remember our faith's promises, principles, and commands. They can also help us cope with negative emotions, temptations, or doubts. We can memorize or recite verses or quotes by writing them down, repeating them aloud, or using apps or flashcards.

- ☐ Do something creative or artistic. Doing something creative or artistic can help us express our faith and connect with our inner self and a higher power. It can also help us relax, have fun, and discover new talents. We can do something creative or artistic by painting, drawing, writing, singing, playing an instrument, or making crafts.

- ☐ Go on a retreat or pilgrimage. Going on a retreat or pilgrimage can help us take a break from our busy and stressful lives and focus on our faith and spiritual growth. It can also help us experience new places, cultures, and people. We can go on a retreat or pilgrimage by joining a group, finding a location, or planning our own itinerary.

- ☐ Fast or abstain from something. Fasting or abstaining from something can help us discipline our Mind, Body, Soul, and Spirit, showing our devotion and obedience to our faith. It can also help us appreciate what we have, detoxify our system, and increase our awareness. We can fast or abstain from something by choosing a time period, a food item, a habit, an activity, or whatever the agreement is between us and our Heavenly Father.

These are a few ways to build your faith and live a more fulfilling life. Try them and see what works best for you. Remember, nothing is set in stone; we are all different, and faith does not happen overnight. It is something that grows over time with practice and perseverance. The more you build your faith, the more you will experience the benefits of living a faithful life.

Once again, faith is not a feeling, a formula, or a fantasy. Actually, it is a confidence-building relationship of trust, knowing, understanding, or journeying. It is an Actionable Process of merging our Heaven on Earth Experiences, allowing us to tap into our *Spirit to Spirit* Relationship with our Heavenly Father or Blueprinted Destiny. Here is what we must know: "*Looking unto Jesus, the author and finisher of our faith, who for the joy that was set before Him endured the cross,* despising the shame, and has sat down at the right hand of the throne of God." Hebrews 12:2. With our *Shield of Faith*, know this:

- ☐ The Blood of Jesus allows us to build our faith in conjunction with the Holy Spirit.

- ☐ The Bible shows us who God is, who He is not, what He has done, what He expects from us, and what to expect from Him.

Why must we know this? In building our faith, *As It Pleases God*, "All Scripture is given by inspiration of God, and is profitable for doctrine, for reproof, for correction, for instruction in righteousness, that the man of God may be complete, thoroughly equipped for every good work." 2 Timothy 3:16-17.

The Helmet of Salvation

In *The WHY Blueprint*, we are almost fully suited with the Whole Armor of God. We already have our *Belt of Truth, Breastplate of Righteousness, Shoes of the Gospel of Peace,* and *Shield of Faith*; it is time to put on the fifth piece of our Spiritual Armor, the *Helmet of Salvation*.

The most predominant question as a Believer is, 'Can we lose our salvation?' The answer is, 'No, we cannot.' We did NOT create salvation; it was NOT derived from our own making, nor were we nailed to a cross for it. God ushered in salvation for us as a standalone GIFT of Spiritual Atonement. Thus, it is not something to lose...it is something to partake in or accept as a FREE WILL Offering from Jesus to make us whole or to heal us through His Blood.

What if we are not empty or sick but Holy Ghost-Filled and Fire-Baptized? Unfortunately, this is not my call to make! Thus, in the Realm of the Spirit, if we do not know who we are, *As It Pleases God*, or living our lives out of purpose...we are not whole. Furthermore, we are indeed Spiritually Sick but do not realize it, or we are lying to ourselves about what is happening within our psyche. To set the record straight: Without our Predestined Blueprint being Spiritually Tilled, *As It Pleases God*, the longing or void will remain, regardless of how we sugarcoat it, them, or that.

More importantly, salvation will never force itself on us; we must come into an AGREEMENT with it. Without the acceptance or agreement, *As It Pleases God*, we become knowingly or unknowingly dangerous, harmful, lethargic, and hopeless to ourselves and others by human default or error. How is this possible, especially when we are Believers? All we need to do is check our fruits.

We are on point if our Spiritual Fruits consist of Love, Joy, Peace, Patience, Kindness, Goodness, Faithfulness, Gentleness, Self-Control, and Christlike behavior. On the other hand, if we are dealing with hate, resentment, sadness, chaos, impatience, rudeness, unfaithfulness, harshness, rebellion, envy, jealousy, greed, pride, coveting, competitiveness, or loose lips, we have work to do!

We often use salvation as a judging factor in Religion; however, in the Eye of God, it is much more profound than that. How so? It is designed to bring us back into our rightful Spiritual Stance with Him.

We are designed to have a *Spirit to Spirit* Relationship with our Heavenly Father. Still, for some reason, we have lost our way back to Spirituality and the knowledge of our Predestined Mission or Blueprint. Without properly intact salvation, *As It Pleases God*, we become subjected to Spiritual Blindness, Deafness, and Muteness with increased battles with the lust of the eyes, the lusts of the flesh, and the pride of life. If one does not believe this, one must check their thoughts! Our mental chatter will tell us everything we need to know, reveal more about what we Do Not want to know, and unveil the lies we tell ourselves.

The power of the mind is neither a joke nor a laughing matter. According to the Heavenly of Heavens, protecting the mind is essential to using salvation as God rightly intended for our well-being and the warring within the psyche. As a Believer, once we understand the *Helmet of Salvation* and what it can do for us, I am sure one would never want to leave home without it or take it for granted.

In times of crisis, suffering, or uncertainty, most would ask, 'What is salvation?' Salvation is derived from the Latin word salvare, which means to save, heal, or deliver. Regardless of what we believe or who we are, the *Helmet of Salvation* is designed to save, heal, and deliver us in the Name of Christ Jesus. In knowing this, salvation does not give us a license to sin beyond measure; it is used to help us amid our repenting, forgiveness, and purging of our weaknesses, traumas, and atrocities.

For the record, if repenting, forgiveness, and purging are not taking place in our lives, it is a possibility that salvation is being misunderstood, misappropriated, or mismanaged. Why? There must be a sacrifice, repentance, forgiveness, correction, and gratefulness where there is sin. So, if the Blood of Jesus is our SACRIFICE, doing His part, we must do ours! It does not matter how often we fail; we must engage in the WHOLE PROCESS without shortchanging ourselves.

Can we save, heal, and deliver ourselves? Yes and No! Yes, we can deliver ourselves based on our present human capacity and limits, doing our part. No, we cannot Spiritually do it Supernaturally without the Holy Trinity involved, or if we are not Spiritually Anointed or Trained. Why? We must involve God in our equational efforts. We do not know how He will use whatever or whomever to manifest or accomplish His Divine Purpose. Furthermore, we do not want to appear manipulative, trying to force the Hand of God without Spiritual Discernment.

Amid our faith, believability, and hope, it is always WISE to involve the *Helmet of Salvation* to get out of our own way, *As It Pleases God*. Why should we wear a helmet that we cannot see, feel, or touch? Simply put, salvation is the act of God's grace that rescues us from sin, death, and the power of evil.

In addition, salvation is not something we can earn, achieve, or deserve by our efforts. Once again, it is a GIFT God offers us freely through our faith in Jesus Christ, who died on the cross for our sins and rose again from the dead to bring us the Comforter (The Holy Spirit). Although we cannot use our physical senses to connect to Him, our Spiritual Senses will do the trick if we allow them to do so. Remember, the Holy Trinity (The Father, Son, and Holy Spirit) is the SALVE we need to soothe the human psyche. All else is irritants without the Trinity.

Salvation is often described as justification, sanctification, and glorification in three aspects: past, present, and future. These simulate the Holy Trinity (The Father, Son, and Holy Spirit), bringing us into our own Spiritual Likeness. What does this mean? We are Spiritual Beings having a human experience. In due season, we are required to operate at our Spiritual Capacity, *As It Pleases God*. If not, the Vicissitudes, Seasons, and Cycles of Life will simulate a déjà vu era, presenting different characters playing their role until we are ready to put on the *Helmet of Salvation*.

Justification

We call dealing with the past aspect of salvation justification. It means God declares us righteous and forgives us of all our sins because of what Christ has done for us. Justification is a legal term implying a CHANGE IN OUR STATUS before God.

We are now accepted, acquitted, and adopted as God's children, causing no one to become an outcast unless they choose to do so. What does this mean? We are no longer guilty or condemned if we REPENT. If we choose not to repent, we become subjected to the repercussions of our omission, commission, or disobedience.

Justification does not exempt us from Seedtime and Harvest, nor does it change our character; however, if we repent, we are offered grace, peace, and mercy to get through whatever, with whomever.

With justification working on our behalf, we must begin to use the Fruits of the Spirit and behave Christlike to place a Spiritual Seal on our STATUS CHANGE. If not, we will begin to work against ourselves inadvertently.

Sanctification

As we look at the present aspect of salvation, it is called sanctification, meaning God makes us HOLY, transforming us into the image of Christ through the vehicle of the Holy Spirit.

Sanctification is a moral term implying a change in our character and conduct; however, we must use the Fruits of the Spirit and behave Christlike. Although we are no longer slaves to sin, selfishness, or worldly desires, we are responsible for using the Spiritual Tools available to keep our Kingdom Status.

What are the Spiritual Tools? There are many Spiritual Tools used for Spiritual Growth; listed below are a few, but not limited to such:

- ☐ Exhibit Love.
- ☐ Pray Without Doing It Amissly.
- ☐ Engage In *Spirit To Spirit* Communion.
- ☐ Reading and Studying The Bible.
- ☐ Fellowship With Other Believers.
- ☐ Worship.
- ☐ Meditation.
- ☐ Repenting, Fasting, and Forgiving.
- ☐ Serving Others and Sharing.
- ☐ Using The Fruits Of The Spirit.
- ☐ Behaving Christlike.
- ☐ Gratitude.
- ☐ Journaling or Documenting *Spirit To Spirit*.
- ☐ Using Our Spiritual Gifts.
- ☐ Putting On The Whole Armor Of God.
- ☐ Avoiding The Things God Hates.
- ☐ Working On Our Predestined Blueprint.

- ☐ Reversing Negatives Into Positives.
- ☐ Create A Win-Win Out Of Everything and With Everyone.
- ☐ Use Positive Affirmations.

Are these really considered Spiritual Tools? Absolutely. They work better than any manmade tools to unveil our Divine Blueprint. How? These Spiritual Tools can help Believers deepen their relationship with God, themselves, and others while growing in faith, stature, and wisdom, *As It Pleases Him*. When used in Spiritually Tilling our own ground, they help us become more effective at being in Purpose on purpose with Spiritual Discernment, putting the enemy at bay.

We can look for the 1-2-3 step or click-our-heels miracle; it does not change our Divine Blueprint or the Spiritual Tools needed. Our step-by-step Blueprint is unique, powerful, impactful, and effective; therefore, we must govern our seeds, roots, and fruits accordingly.

What if we engage in bad works amid our sanctification stage and avoid using Spiritual Tools? The goal is to become a work-in-progress for the greater good and to create a win-win out of everything and with everyone. Unfortunately, we do not come straight out of the gate perfect, nor are we perfect in the Eye of God; however, He watches our fruits, motives, and character. Here is the deal: If they remain the same or worsen without improving, we will get a Kingdomly Side-Eye.

More importantly, in our desire for wholeness, healing, and safety, He notes whether we abuse the Spiritual System designed to help us in those areas. When we engage in bad works amid our sanctification stage, we are hurting ourselves and grieving the Holy Spirit who dwells in us, quenching His power and influence in our lives. Frankly, the last thing we want to do is turn against the Holy Trinity or ourselves. Why? The next phase of our salvation depends on it.

Glorification

The future aspect of salvation is called glorification. Glorification means God will complete the work of salvation in us when Christ returns and gives us new bodies free from sickness, pain, and death. And we are no longer subject to decay, corruption, or destruction.

One of the most anticipated events in Christian eschatology is the second coming of Jesus Christ. According to the Bible, Jesus will return to earth in glory and power, accompanied by His Angels, to judge the living and the dead and to establish His Kingdom. By the time we reach this point, the goal is to possess Christlike Characteristics with the active use of the Fruits of the Spirit. Is there any other way? There are many ways in the Eye of God; however, it is best to remain with the surefire way, using the Fruits of the Spirit and behaving Christlike across the board.

When the time comes, we do not want to figure things out or search for oil; we want to be in the number with our Spiritual Lamps ready or our Spiritual Oil overstocked. What does this mean? We must work on ourselves daily without waiting until the last minute to work on our pride, envy, jealousy, greed, coveting, anger, resentment, unforgiveness, and so on.

Once again, do not think salvation is a license to sin; it is the license to work on ourselves to get in Divine Alignment, *As It Pleases God*, and bring ourselves in Purpose on purpose. Here is what we must know: *"And the nations of those who are saved shall walk in its light, and the kings of the earth bring their glory and honor into it. Its gates shall not be shut at all by day (there shall be no night there). And they shall bring the glory and the honor of the nations into it. But there shall by no means enter it anything that defiles, or causes an abomination or a lie, but only those who are written in the Lamb's Book of Life."* Revelation 21:24-27. When dealing with the *Helmet of Salvation*, if we want life, give it. If we are the Lamb's Book of Life, our TESTIMONY should reveal it.

What is the Lamb's Book of Life, and why is it important? First, the Lamb's Book of Life is a Biblical term referring to a HEAVENLY RECORD of all those who have trusted in Jesus Christ for salvation. Secondly, the Lamb's Book of Life is also called the Book of Life, the Book of the Living, or the Book of Remembrance. Why is this so important? It is first mentioned in Exodus 32:32-33, where Moses intercedes for the Israelites after they worshiped the golden calf. He asks God to forgive their sin or blot him out of the book God has written. God replies that He will blot out whoever has sinned against Him from His book, signifying the importance of REPENTING.

Can God hear our petitions when interceding? Of course. When we possess fear and reverence, *As It Pleases Him*, He will move Heaven and Earth for us. He will speak, and we will hear Him. *"Then those who feared the Lord spoke to one another, And the Lord listened and heard them; So a book of remembrance was written before Him For those who fear the Lord And who meditate on His name."* Malachi 3:16.

The WHY Blueprint

The Bible teaches that when Jesus comes again, He will transform the bodies of His faithful followers into glorious, immortal, and incorruptible bodies, called the Glorification of the Saints. The apostle Paul documents in 1 Corinthians 15:51-53: *"Behold, I tell you a mystery: We shall not all sleep, but we shall all be changed— in a moment, in the twinkling of an eye, at the last trumpet. For the trumpet will sound, and the dead will be raised incorruptible, and we shall be changed. For this corruptible must put on incorruption, and this mortal must put on immortality."*

The Glorification of the Saints is the final stage of our salvation. Is this Biblical? *"Moreover whom He predestined, these He also called; whom He called, these He also justified; and whom He justified, these He also glorified."* Romans 8:30. God not only calls and justifies but also glorifies us. If we put on the *Helmet of Salvation*, using it as a Spiritual Tool, *As It Pleases God*, it will guide us on what to do and what not to do, especially if we have Spiritual Ears to hear.

Having Spiritual Ears means hearing the Voice of God and discerning His Divine Will, Nudges, and Direction. According to the Heavenly of Heavens, it requires tuning out the worldly distractions and being open to the guidance of the Holy Spirit. By cultivating a habit of prayer, spending time in God's Word, and engaging in *Spirit to Spirit* Communion, we can develop our Spiritual Eyes, Ears, and Tongues.

To achieve ONENESS with God and our Eternal Life in Heaven are the ultimate goals of all Believers. *"For our citizenship is in heaven, from which we also eagerly wait for the Savior, the Lord Jesus Christ, who will transform our lowly body that it may be conformed to His glorious body, according to the working by which He is able even to subdue all things to Himself."* Philippians 3:20-21. Amid all, it is imperative to MASTER the ability to glorify

God, *As It Pleases Him*. Why must we master this? Often, we pick and choose what we think He wants from us; yet for a time such as this, He has zero tolerance for not being in the Spiritual Know, especially when it is documented in the Bible.

As Believers, we are called to glorify God in everything we do. In dealing with the *Whole Armor of God*, glorification is established through our thoughts, words, and actions to bring glory to Him or to deflate our relationship with Him. All of which are revealed in our character, fruits, reactions, and demeanor.

How do we glorify God in our thoughts? Our thoughts are the melting pot of our attitudes, emotions, biases, traumas, habits, and actions. With this mixture, we must align our thoughts with God's Divine Truth and Wisdom instead of resorting to folly. Why must we incorporate Divine Truth and Wisdom? Simply put, lies, debauchery, and folly are a recipe for disaster. How? The ungoverned, unchecked, or mismanaged mental chatter is getting the best of us, thwarting the psyche beyond measure.

Unbeknown to most, even if we have self-control, the mind chats on unless we change the channel. Then again, most DO NOT know how to change the channel, and we have some who ENJOY the feedback. Who knows, right? We can glorify God in our thoughts by:

- ☐ Meditating on His Word, attributes, and character. Spending time thinking about God's love, grace, mercy, and faithfulness plants good seeds in the Mind, Body, Soul, and Spirit. The Bible is the decisive source of truth and guidance for our lives, even if we do not fully understand everything. Still, read it daily, study it carefully, memorize it faithfully, and apply it diligently. The understanding will come; we just need to remain consistent. *"And do not be conformed to this world, but be transformed by the renewing of your mind, that you may prove what is that good and acceptable and perfect will of God."* Romans 12:2.

- [ ] Fill your mind with Biblical Truth and positive affirmations, allowing it to shape your thinking. We should fill our minds with positive, edifying thoughts reflecting God's Divine Character and Will. We should avoid dwelling on negative and sinful thoughts that dishonor Him and lead us astray. *"Finally, brethren, whatever things are true, whatever things are noble, whatever things are just, whatever things are pure, whatever things are lovely, whatever things are of good report, if there is any virtue and if there is anything praiseworthy—meditate on these things."* Philippians 4:8.

- [ ] Cultivate a Spirit of Gratitude. Here is the secret: Focus on the good things in your life and thank God for all things, the good, bad, or indifferent. *"In everything, give thanks; for this is the will of God in Christ Jesus for you."* 1 Thessalonians 5:18.

- [ ] Praying without ceasing. Prayer is how we communicate with God and express our dependence on Him. *"Pray without ceasing."* 1 Thessalonians 5:17.

- [ ] Our thoughts have a powerful impact on us. By intentionally redirecting them toward the Word of God along with positivity, righteousness, and fruitfulness, we can honor Him in all areas of our lives WITHOUT being so Heavenly Minded that we are no earthly good. What does this mean? We are relatable and relevant, *As It Pleases God*, without hitting people over the head with the Bible.

Should we not spread the Word of God? Absolutely! We must share the Good News. Inarguably, we must ensure we are first spreading the Fruits of the Spirit and Christlike Character. Why? There is NO LAW against the Fruits of the Spirit, and they speak for themselves. Blasphemy, right? Wrong! *"The Lord has appeared of old to me, saying: 'Yes, I have loved you with an everlasting love; Therefore with lovingkindness I have drawn you.'"* Jeremiah 31:3.

How do we glorify God in our words? In the Eye of God, we must use our words wisely and graciously. Why should we become cautious with our words? *"Death and life are in the power of the tongue, And those who love it will eat its fruit."* Proverbs 18:21. Here are some ways we can glorify God in our words:

- ☐ Speak words of encouragement and kindness. We can use our words to lift others up, building their faith. *"Pleasant words are like a honeycomb, Sweetness to the soul and health to the bones."* Proverbs 16:24.

- ☐ Avoid gossip, slander, and negative speech. Instead of tearing others down, we should speak words to enlighten and bring people closer together. *"Let no corrupt communication proceed out of your mouth, but that which is good to the use of edifying, that it may minister grace unto the hearers."* Ephesians 4:29.

- ☐ Speak the truth in love. We should always be truthful, mindful of how we say things, and make sure our words are spoken lovingly, gently, and respectfully. *"But speaking the truth in love, may grow up into Him in all things."* Ephesians 4:15.

- ☐ Give thanks and praise to God. We can use our words to express our gratitude and worship to God, giving Him the glory and honor He deserves. Here is a ONE-UP: God likes a sweet mouth...this is one of the reasons King David was after God's heart. *"How sweet are Your words to my taste, Sweeter than honey to my mouth!"* Psalm 119:103.

By using our words to glorify God, we can positively impact the world around us and honor the One who created us. How do we glorify Him, especially if we are not after His heart and have issues? As Believers, we are called to glorify God not only in our thoughts or words, but also in our actions. For this reason, regardless of where we are in our Spiritual Relationship with Him, if we begin consciously using the Fruits of the Spirit and behaving Christlike, we can get the ball rolling with the words, thoughts, and actions pleasing Him.

Our actions can be powerful witnesses to those around us, reflecting our love for God and obedience to Him. On the other hand, it can also reflect our folly, disobedience, rebellion, selfishness, and so on. For example, I pay close attention to what people SAY and DO. Why? It reveals their fruits, even if they are operating under a massive cover-up or disguise. Here are some ways to glorify God in our actions:

- ☐ Serve others. Jesus taught us that the greatest among us should be the servant of all. We can glorify God by serving others and meeting their needs.

- ☐ Live a Holy life. We are called to be set apart from the world and live a life that honors God. By making choices consistent with God's Divine Will, we can glorify Him in our actions.

- ☐ Share the Gospel. We can glorify God by sharing the good news of Jesus Christ with others and living a life that reflects the truth of the Gospel.

- ☐ Use our talents and abilities for God's glory, according to our Predestined Blueprint. God has given each of us unique Talents, Gifts, Skills, Creativity, and Purpose, and we can use them to bring glory to Him. We can use our gifts to honor God through music, art, writing, or other forms of creativity.

- ☐ Love others. Jesus taught us to love our neighbors as ourselves. By showing love and compassion to those around us, we can glorify God and reflect His character to the world. By living a life that glorifies God in our actions, we can make a difference in the world and be a powerful witness to those around us.

To glorify God is to honor, praise, and magnify Him, *As It Pleases Him*, not as it pleases us. Although our Spiritual Relationships are personal, our glorification should at least acknowledge His greatness, goodness, mercy, love, and grace while living by example. Here is the Spiritual Seal: *"The things which you learned and received and heard and saw in me, these do, and the God of peace will be with you."* Philippians 4:9.

Knowing what you now know, you can use the *Helmet of Salvation* as a Spiritual Symbol of submission and respect for Divine Authority. And when you *"Submit yourselves therefore to God. Resist the devil, and he will flee from you."* James 4:7.

The Sword of The Spirit

As we are now fully suited with our *Belt of Truth*, the *Breastplate of Righteousness*, the *Shoes of the Gospel of Peace*, the *Shield of Faith*, and our *Helmet of Salvation*, let us pick up the sixth piece of the armor, the *Sword of the Spirit*. According to the Heavenly of Heavens, this is an excellent way to Spiritually Gear up every morning and lay our Spiritual Armor down at night before bed with a Mental Picture in our Mind's Eye. Does it work? It depends on our faith! In the same way, we picture having a cup of coffee before making it; we can put on or take off our Spiritual Armor. Let me show you how to work it, *As It Pleases God*.

The *Sword of the Spirit* is the only offensive piece of Spiritual Armor that Paul mentions in Ephesians 6:10-18, where he instructs the believers to put on the *Whole Armor of God* to stand against the devil's schemes. The other armor pieces are defensive, such as the Belt of Truth, our Breastplate of Righteousness, our Shield of Faith, our Helmet of Salvation, and our Shoes of Peace. These are meant to protect us from enemy attacks and those who try to deceive, accuse, tempt, manipulate, bully, and discourage us. The *Sword of the Spirit* differs from all the Spiritual Tools or Weapons. It is not only for defense but also for offense, enabling us to resist and defeat the enemy.

The *Sword of the Spirit* is the Word of God. How can the Word of God become our sword? According to scripture, *"For the word of God is living and powerful, and sharper than any two-edged sword, piercing even to the division of soul and spirit, and of joints and marrow, and is a discerner of the thoughts and intents of the heart."* Hebrews 4:12.

The Word of God is powerful and effective, cutting through the lies, doubts, fears, or sins hindering us from following His Divine Will. How so? Once again, *"All Scripture is given by inspiration of God, and is profitable for doctrine, for reproof, for correction, for instruction in righteousness, that the man of God may be complete, thoroughly equipped for every good work."* 2 Timothy 3:16-17. Unbeknown to most, it is a weapon against the enemy and a regrafting tool for our growth, tilling, and transformation.

The *Sword of the Spirit* is also a weapon we can use in prayer to back up our Spiritual Claims to our Heavenly Father. When dealing with the *Whole Armor of God*, if we desire to Spiritually Enforce ourselves against the enemy's wiles, we must use the Word of God as ammunition, casting it, them, or that down with Spiritual Reinforcement at our beck and call.

For starters, once we place God first in our lives, *As It Pleases Him*. He is 100% for us because we have removed selfishness, disobedience, and rebellion from the equation. Secondly, the moment we use the Blood of Jesus as our Spiritual Atonement, repenting of our sins and forgiving everyone, the Blood Covering becomes Spiritually Active. Thirdly, our sword becomes HOT when we AWAKEN our Spirit to become ONE with the Holy Spirit. By having the combination of the Holy Trinity working on our behalf, we are much stronger than someone who does nothing or thinks they are a one-pony rodeo.

Unfortunately, most Believers stop at the Holy Trinity and become powerless or too Religious, not realizing the Fruits of the Spirit are designed to fuel the fire behind the *Sword of the Spirit*. What is the purpose of this happening? Let me counteract this question with another. How can we take down the enemy when we are behaving like them? How can we cast down something or someone when we are guilty of the same things under a different label? How can we contend with the enemy with rotten and mangled fruits? Bottom line, we must use the Fruits of the Spirit and behave Christlike; if not, the Holy Spirit must lie dormant. Why? He will not operate in our folly!

On the other hand, if we become an ACTIVE work-in-progress, making our best attempt to use the Fruits of the Spirit and behave Christlike, He will work with us in a Spiritual Classroom setup, guiding, protecting, and training us. More importantly, it comes with a layer of Spiritual Protection because we are students in training.

When we are in a student-teacher relationship with the guidance of the Holy Spirit covered by the Blood of Jesus, the Teach Me, Show Me, Guide Me, Lead Me, and Help Me prefaces carry Kingdom Weight beyond human reasoning, giving our *Sword of the Spirit* a little more fire. If one does not believe this, they have the free will to TEST THE SPIRIT in this area.

Above all, once we connect to our reason for being or Divine Blueprint, it comes with Divine Protection from the Four Corners, getting us ready for whatever with whomever. Remember that no one has the exact Spiritual Blueprint or the primal details outside the Holy Trinity and the BLUEPRINTED individual. More importantly, it is

Spiritually Guarded and kept under a locking key until we are ready for training.

How do we unlock our Blueprint? We must go through the one Who gave us the Spiritual Assignment—God Almighty. Nevertheless, once we are in Purpose on purpose, *As It Pleases Him*, it comes with Supernatural Protection, giving our *Sword of the Spirit* more fire with a Spiritual Seal. Is this Biblical? I would have it no other way. "*After these things I saw four angels standing at the four corners of the earth, holding the four winds of the earth, that the wind should not blow on the earth, on the sea, or on any tree. Then I saw another angel ascending from the east, having the seal of the living God. And he cried with a loud voice to the four angels to whom it was granted to harm the earth and the sea, saying, 'Do not harm the earth, the sea, or the trees till we have sealed the servants of our God on their foreheads.'*" Revelation 7:1-3.

Once we possess a Spiritual Sword or Seal, we must also be careful not to misuse or abuse it. We should not twist it or take it out of context to suit our own agenda or preferences. We should not use it to hurt or condemn others, but to edify and encourage them. We should not use it as a weapon of pride or self-righteousness; it is designed to advance God's Kingdom and fulfill His Divine Purposes, *As It Pleases Him*.

The Whole Armor of God

Once we have adorned ourselves with our Spiritual Armor, we must prepare ourselves to carry the weight of it. By putting on *The Whole Armor of God*, we are not only preparing ourselves for Spiritual Warfare, but also expressing our identity as God's sheep, children, or servants, depending on Him.

For example, a young man named Jack was facing many challenges and hardships, battling with the cycle of déjà vu. He struggled with his studies, relationships, and personal life, serving him a bitter portion of rotten fruit. As a result, he felt lost, faithless, and hopeless, and he did not know what to do or who to turn to, feeling like God had turned His back on him.

One day, Jack's grandmother visited him and saw how troubled he was. She knew exactly what he needed, and she took out her Bible and read to him about *The Whole Armor of God*. She explained to Jack that just like a soldier needs armor to protect himself in battle, he must also put on *The Whole Armor of God* to protect himself from life's trials, vicissitudes, and challenges.

She explained how to practically use his Belt of Truth, Breastplate of Righteousness, Shoes of Peace, Shield of Faith, Helmet of Salvation, and the Sword of the Spirit. Then she taught him about combining them with the Fruits of the Spirit while apologizing for not teaching him about the Spiritual Tools earlier.

Jack was initially skeptical, but his grandmother's words resonated with him, penetrating the core of his being, knowing she would not mislead him. As a commitment to himself, he decided to put on *The Whole Armor of God* piece by piece, Mentally, Emotionally, and Spiritually, while using the Fruits of the Spirit for forty days to see what would happen.

He started reading his Bible every day and praying for strength and guidance. As time went by, Jack noticed a change in himself. He felt more confident and peaceful, facing his challenges with courage and faith. He realized that *The Whole Armor of God* was not just a metaphor but a real source of strength and protection, and the Fruits of the Spirit really worked in updating his people skills.

From the fortieth day onward, Jack made a lifetime commitment to put on *The Whole Armor of God* every day and use the Fruits of the Spirit, even when it did not make sense to use them. Although he knew that life would always have its challenges, he was confident that with God's help, he could overcome them all. He was grateful to his grandmother for showing him the way, and he knew that the power of The Holy Trinity would always guide him. By all means, this one act of obedience changed the trajectory of his life.

Jack is happily married with five children and has a Doctorate Degree in Science, placing a Spiritual Seal on *The WHY Blueprint*. Above all, he learned that 'What Hurts You is What Heals You,' especially if you learn how to use the Spiritual Tools, *As It Pleases God*. More importantly, although he was delayed, he was not denied; as a result, he teaches his children these Spiritual Principles at a young age to avoid a Bloodline delay, building their positive character traits, fruits, and internal security early.

Chapter Ten
Overcoming Insecurity

When dealing with *The WHY Blueprint*, overcoming insecurities from the inside out is imperative, *As It Pleases God*. Our Gifts, Calling, Talents, and Creativity are often wrapped in our weaknesses, traumas, or insecurities. Suppose we are in denial or refuse to learn from it or them. In this case, we often do not receive the benefits or extract the Divine Blessings hidden within whatever or with whomever. Then again, we sometimes miss the Spiritual Classroom altogether.

When we think about insecurity, we often revert to the negative side, overlooking the positive, mainly when we only need an understanding of effective communication and its expectations. How can insecurity be positive, especially when negative stipulations are apparent? If we are not insecure at some point in our lives, we will not know the difference between humility and confidence, *As It Pleases God*.

Without whitewashing insecurity, we often do not succeed because we have not learned how to articulate or document our wants, needs, and desires. As a result, we fall short, not knowing why, while absorbing a blow to the ego. With *The WHY Blueprint*, we must leave no stone unturned. Why? There is a win-win hidden within everything and with everyone, and it is your responsibility to pinpoint it, them, or that, ensuring '*What Hurts You is What Heals You.*'

Insecurity can significantly impact the psyche, leading to low self-esteem, anxiety, trauma, depression, and split personality disorders. It can also perpetuate negative behaviors, such as people-pleasing, seeking validation from others, judging people, places, and things, complaining about everything, or outright bullying others. Addressing our insecurities can involve:

- ☐ Therapy.
- ☐ Building self-awareness.
- ☐ Working on self-acceptance and self-love.
- ☐ Developing a *Spirit to Spirit* Relationship with our Heavenly Father.

If we avoid seeking help, avoid correction, or refuse to repent, narcissism, paranoia, doubt, and phobias are on the horizon. Really? Yes, really! Unfortunately, it is the cover-up and pretense that gets us, causing varying phobias and vast paranoias, perpetuating all the other negative characteristics.

Are our phobias and paranoia the same? They are different but often intertwined together like cousins. Paranoia is a mental disorder causing delusions of persecution, suspicion, and mistrust of others. A phobia is an irrational fear of a specific person, place, thing, object, situation, or activity that interferes with our daily lives. All are due to the lack of repentance, unhealed narcissism, stiff-necked disobedience, unrecognized trauma, or unresolved doubt.

Regardless of where we are on our Spiritual Journey, it is important to remember that everyone has insecurities, and it is okay to ask for help addressing them. By addressing our insecurities or knowing what to do about them, we can improve ourselves Mentally, Physically, Emotionally, and Spiritually, *As It Pleases God*.

In the Eye of God, we should not be walking around pretending we have it all together when we do not. The lies we tell ourselves are the same ones that will destroy us, especially if we do not get our acts together, *As It Pleases Him*. Here are a few ways to overcome our insecurities with *The WHY Blueprint*, but not limited to such:

- ☐ Use the Word of God, quoting relevant scriptures back to Him and ourselves.
- ☐ Practice positive self-affirmations and self-talk, casting down any form of negativity.
- ☐ Surround yourself with positive people, places, and things.
- ☐ Identify your negative triggers and overcome them, leaving no stone unturned.
- ☐ Focus on your strengths and accomplishments with outright humility.
- ☐ Challenge your negative thoughts, actions, and beliefs with the Fruits of the Spirit.
- ☐ Set achievable goals and celebrate your progress.
- ☐ Learn to accept and give compliments graciously.
- ☐ Do not compare yourself to others or engage in competitiveness.
- ☐ Learn to say NO and set boundaries.

- ☐ Do not allow fear to keep you from trying new things while exercising wisdom.
- ☐ Practice gratitude, giving thanks in all things.
- ☐ Practice forgiveness, both towards yourself and others, without pointing the finger.
- ☐ Seek out positive role models, and work toward becoming one yourself.
- ☐ Volunteer or help others in need, activating the Law of Reciprocity.
- ☐ Look for opportunities to learn and improve yourself by becoming a work-in-progress.
- ☐ Feel free to ask for help when you need it.
- ☐ Take time for yourself and do the things you enjoy.
- ☐ Embrace your uniqueness and individuality.
- ☐ Do not let others' opinions define you.
- ☐ Learn to trust yourself and your decisions.
- ☐ Overcome doubt and second-guessing yourself by planning your actions, thoughts, or beliefs.
- ☐ Stay away from toxic relationships, triggers, and situations.
- ☐ Be kind to yourself and others.
- ☐ Treat yourself and others with respect.
- ☐ Do not allow your past mistakes to define you negatively. They are lessons and stepping stones that will take you to the next level.
- ☐ Focus on your progress rather than perfection.
- ☐ Learn to handle constructive criticism without taking it personally.
- ☐ Do not let your fear of failure keep you from pursuing your goals. Keep it moving in the Spirit of Excellence.
- ☐ Be patient with yourself and your progress, taking one step at a time.
- ☐ Take responsibility for yourself and your decisions, even if they are not your fault. Life has to yield a

lesson when you take responsibility to grow, learn, and share.
- ☐ Do not allow setbacks to discourage you from continuing to try.
- ☐ Learn to communicate effectively with others, mastering your people skills.
- ☐ Seek out a mentor, counselor, or coach for guidance and support.
- ☐ Take time to rest and recharge regularly.
- ☐ Learn to let go of what you cannot control.
- ☐ Surround yourself with positive and uplifting media.
- ☐ Learn to appreciate and celebrate others' successes.
- ☐ Focus on your personal growth and development.
- ☐ Do not let fear of rejection hold you back from pursuing relationships.

Can this list really help us? Absolutely. We cannot just wing it when dealing with known or unknown insecurities. The human psyche is too intelligent to fool; we need to implement positive actions, thoughts, and beliefs, causing the adaptation phase to occur without going cold turkey.

Introducing the psyche to positivity slowly and continuously will cause it to respond advantageously. This introductory phase is similar to taking a baby from milk to soft foods and from soft foods to solids. On the other hand, if we begin to rule the psyche with an iron sword, it may fight us back or traumatize us, causing lapses of shame, similar to going from sinner to saint overnight.

No judgment is intended; I must deliver the Divine Message. The worldly mentality does not evaporate; it must be Spiritually Regrafted and Pruned. If not, we will take this same mentality, putting a little Jesus on it and serving it to others without any Spiritual Training, Principles, or

Understanding. For this reason, the work-in-progress mentality, *As It Pleases God*, works best for us and avoids inner confusion, allowing our conscience to work effectively.

What does inner confusion have to do with our psyche? Inner confusion refers to mental disarray or uncertainty arising from conflicting thoughts, emotions, actions, or beliefs. It can be a challenging and uncomfortable experience, making it difficult to make decisions, remain focused, and feel a sense of inner peace.

Inner confusion can arise from various factors, including stress, anxiety, depression, rebellion, or simply from feeling overwhelmed by life's demands. Acknowledging and addressing this issue without sweeping it under the rug is essential. Aside from the list above, please make sure you are doing three things:

- ☐ Write down your thoughts and feelings in your Spiritual Journal.
- ☐ List your positive attributes and refer to them to reset your mindset daily.
- ☐ List things that make you happy and refer to them often.

Why do we need to journal this information? When we journal, we can reflect on things we may have forgotten or overlooked and create a track record of our growth process.

Some people keep a Spiritual Journal, while others opt for a regular journal. What is the difference? A Spiritual Journal typically focuses on exploring one's relationship with God Almighty or finding meaning in life. It may include prayers, meditations, Spiritual Decrees, Spiritual Reflections, or Spiritual Writings.

On the other hand, a regular journal can be more general and cover a range of topics, from daily activities to personal growth, love life, and so on. Ultimately, the type of journal you choose to keep depends on your personal preferences and goals. Whether you choose a Spiritual or regular journal, writing can be a powerful tool for self-discovery and growth. It may also become a book to share with others. Nonetheless, here are a few reasons to keep a Spiritual Journal or regular journal, but not limited to such:

- ☐ Journals help us to organize our thoughts and ideas.
- ☐ They enable us to track our progress and growth.
- ☐ Writing in a journal can be Spiritually Therapeutic and help us process our emotions, actions, thoughts, beliefs, and biases.
- ☐ Journals provide a safe space to express ourselves without fear of judgment or criticism.
- ☐ They help us to remember important details and experiences.
- ☐ Journals can serve as a creative outlet for writers and artists.
- ☐ They can aid in problem-solving and decision-making.
- ☐ Journals can help us to set and achieve goals.
- ☐ They allow us to reflect on and learn from past experiences.
- ☐ Journals can be used to document our daily routines and habits.
- ☐ Writing in a journal can improve our writing skills.
- ☐ Journals help us stay accountable and motivated.
- ☐ They can serve as a record of our personal history and legacy.
- ☐ Journals can be used to brainstorm and generate new ideas.

- ☐ They can help us to clarify our thoughts and beliefs.
- ☐ Journals can be a tool for self-discovery and self-improvement.
- ☐ They allow us to explore our creativity and imagination.
- ☐ Journals can be used for academic and professional purposes.
- ☐ They can help us develop better communication skills.
- ☐ Journals can provide a sense of closure and resolution to challenging experiences.

Developing a strong and healthy relationship with God, ourselves, and others requires effort, commitment, and documentation. One way to address the root cause of relationship insecurity is by fostering open and honest communication.

Actively listening to each other's concerns, needs, wants, and desires while respecting each other's boundaries creates strong bonds. Does this apply to our Godly or *Spirit to Spirit* Relations? Yes. Trust and respect are vital in creating a solid foundation with God, ourselves, and others, even if we do not believe, have faith, lack understanding, or wallow in a bed of doubt. Unfortunately, according to our Predestined Blueprint, it does not change our Spiritual Expectations or Blueprint.

Taking responsibility for our actions, thoughts, and emotions can help prevent insecurities from arising in the first place, allowing us to become more present and grounded in our relationships. On the other hand, if we think we are above God, we will become narcissists by default, causing us to sabotage relationships, situations, circumstances, and events to exemplify our worthiness.

What is narcissism? Narcissism is an underlying personality disorder characterized by a sense of self-importance, a need for admiration, and a lack of empathy for others. Individuals with narcissistic tendencies often have an inflated sense of self-worth and a lack of humility, believing they are entitled to special treatment. Unfortunately, this person may also struggle to accept criticism or feedback while failing to maintain healthy relationships, thinking everyone else has the problem.

On the other hand, they may be a master manipulator playing dumb. What does this mean? While everyone is laughing at their lack of cleverness, they have indeed outsmarted and outplotted the ones laughing. How is this possible? It is achieved through reverse psychology. The moment we allow laughter to tickle our fancy is when we 'get got' by their antics, allowing them to cover their tracks through the battle of wits. When dealing with this type of individual, their dumbed-down riddles are actually a plan hidden in plain sight.

Sober up, my friends, especially when dealing with a narcissist. Their plans are well thought out to unsmart the seemingly smart, deflecting the heat from one place to another! How can we avoid this pitfall? Test the Spirit! How? First, cast down the Spirit of Deception and usher in the Spirit of Discernment, allowing the scales to fall off. Secondly, plead the Blood of Jesus or say, 'Deceptive Spirit, the Blood is against you.' Thirdly, usher in the Holy Spirit for Divine Revelation. Fourthly, wait for the information and document.

Why is it essential to test the Spirit? It is done to protect yourself and your sanity. A relationship with a narcissist can have serious long-term consequences, including emotional trauma, anxiety, and depression. It can also lead to a cycle of abuse, bullying, and manipulation that can be difficult to break free from.

Some evidence suggests that there may be a genetic component to narcissism. Still, environmental factors such as childhood trauma, parenting style, abandonment, and abuse play a significant role in developing narcissistic tendencies.

For example, John was obsessed with his appearance, thinking he was God's gift to women. He would spend hours in front of the mirror, admiring his good looks, and often take selfies to post on social media for likes and comments to satiate his ego before leaving home.

John's friends and family members were worried about his excessive pompousness, while at the same time, cringing because of his flashiness. Although he felt the tension, he brushed off their concerns as if they were envious of him and his lifestyle. Due to his family not feeding his ego, he constantly sought validation from others, getting upset if he did not receive compliments throughout the day.

One day, John met a girl named Sarah, who was everything he ever wanted in a partner. She was beautiful, intelligent, and kind. However, as their relationship progressed, John's narcissistic tendencies started to show. He would constantly talk about himself and his accomplishments and belittle Sarah's achievements as if she were a nobody. Adding insult to injury, he would also get upset if she did not give him enough attention and would accuse her of not loving him. He also used his relations with other women to make her jealous, provoking her to bow down to him and for ultimate control.

Eventually, Sarah had had enough of his pathological lying and decided to end the relationship after she became Mentally, Physically, Emotionally, and Spiritually exhausted. John was devastated, but instead of reflecting on his behavior, he blamed Sarah for not appreciating him enough. As time passed, John's narcissism grew worse: overbearing, abusive, unregulated, and toxic.

Not only did he lose Sarah, but he also lost many friendships and job opportunities because of his self-centered attitude and pompousness. Unfortunately, he ended up alone and unhappy while using his negative habits to keep him grounded. To say the least, He blamed God for his recklessness and categorized all women for his unresolved or deflected issues.

In the end, John realizes his obsession with his appearance and need for validation have caused him to lose everything he ever wanted. As the tables turned as they always do, He consciously changed his narcissistic ways, focusing on building genuine relationships using the Fruits of the Spirit and Christlike Character without judging anyone, seeking attention, or receiving validation from others. More importantly, he began to live his life, *As It Pleased God*, taking one day at a time. And now, 'What Hurt Him is What Healed Him.'

The story of John reminds us of the dangers of excessive self-love and its negative impact. However, becoming obsessed with our appearance and seeking validation from others is easy. But true joy, happiness, and fulfillment come from building sincere connections with God, ourselves, and others, in this Divine Order.

Let John's story inspire us to reflect on our own behaviors, striving to be more humble, kind, and empathetic towards others using the Fruits of the Spirit and exhibiting Christlike Character, *As It Pleases God.*

Kingdom Confidence

With *The WHY Blueprint*, it is imperative to walk confidently, think the right thoughts, do the right things, say what is good, pleasant, and pleasing to God and ourselves, and become all God has created for us to become.

According to the Heavenly of Heavens, *Kingdom Confidence* should not be taken for granted, placed on display, or abused; it is an INSIDE JOB, radiating outwardly, *As It Pleases God*. "For the LORD will be your confidence, And will keep your foot from being caught." Proverbs 3:26.

Kingdom Confidence is developed by confiding in God Almighty, *Spirit to Spirit*. Why? Worldly confidence can only take us so far, making it easy to lie to God, ourselves, and others, zapping our authenticity and causing us to waver. All these make it possible to put on the *Whole Armor of God*, shaking in our boots with insecurity. When this happens, it does not make us a bad person, unfaithful, unworthy, or unusable...it makes us susceptible to becoming a prime target, easily dismantled, shamingly outed, or pit maneuvered. This analogy resembles how Joseph's brothers threw him into a pit in Genesis 37:23-26, "*So it came to pass, when Joseph had come to his brothers, that they stripped Joseph of his tunic, the tunic of many colors that was on him. Then they took him and cast him into a pit. And the pit was empty; there was no water in it.*"

We never want to give the enemy easy access; he must work for his keep! With *Kingdom Confidence*, the goal is to "Let God be true but every man a liar. As it is written: 'That You may be justified in Your words, and may overcome when You are judged.' " Romans 3:4.

How do we extract the truth, especially when lies surround us? We must seek Divine Truth and the Hand of God while intentionally targeting our Predestined

Blueprinted Mission. Why? It helps us to become Spiritually Aligned and Trained, *As It Pleases God*. As long as we become repentingly and humbly ONE with the Holy Trinity, put on the *Whole Armor of God*, use the Fruits of the Spirit, and behave Christlike to the best of our ability, we have the Spiritual Right to seek the Hand of God without it smiting us.

Why would the *Hand of God* smite us? It will vary from person to person, situation to situation, event to event, culture to culture, condition to condition, trauma to trauma, and so on. However, our motives are vital from our hands to His, and vice versa, which we will discuss further in the next chapter.

We all have issues and must deal with something or someone; the goal is to become and remain JUST in our doings, sayings, and becoming. Here is why: "*The curse of the LORD is on the house of the wicked, But He blesses the home of the just.*" Proverbs 3:33. We can justify, rationalize, and Spiritualize this all we like, but our seeds, fruits, and roots DO NOT lie! They never have and never will...so it behooves us to use the Spiritual Tools available to us, *As It Pleases God*, and not as it pleases ourselves.

CHAPTER ELEVEN
The Lord Will Provide

Have you ever wondered about the Supreme Power of God's Mighty Hand? Is it a literal hand, like ours, or a metaphorical one, representing His Divine Power, Glory, and Authority? Then again, we may also ask, 'Will God really provide for us?' As humans, we tend to question these things without verbalizing our qualms or queries, pretending we do not. And it is perfectly okay; life happens to us all, which is why we need FAITH.

The *Hand of God* is not only a way of describing what God does through love, wisdom, and justice, but also who He is in us, through us, and around us. Will He really speak to us? Absolutely! *"The heavens declare the glory of God; and the firmament shows His handiwork. Day unto day utters speech, And night unto night reveals knowledge. There is no speech nor language where their voice is not heard."* Psalm 19:1-3. However, preparation is needed, similar to how Moses prepared the Children of Israel to meet with God in Exodus 19.

According to our Predestined Blueprint, the *Hand of God* is open to us with the *Kingdom Confidence* needed; however, we must know how to gain Divine Access. Having the *Hand of God* move in our favor is a sought-after experience by most, but experienced by few. Nevertheless, if this book is in your hands, you are included in the few. *"Therefore humble yourselves under the mighty Hand of God, that He may exalt you in due time, casting all your care upon Him, for He cares for you."* 1 Peter 5:6-7.

We often look for Divine Intervention and Miracles, but forget what it takes to POSITION ourselves to receive, handle, or share. The unseen force guiding our lives is not something we should downplay; they all work together for our good if we allow them.

The Lord Will Provide Mindset or Heart Posture is not something we should take for granted. Why? It contains the Divine Provisions for our Predestined Blueprint. Of course, money will not rain down from the Heavenly of Heavens. Still, He will provide the Spiritual Tools, resources, connections, underground reserves, or whatever to bring our Divine Blueprint to life.

The WHY Blueprint is based upon *The LORD-Will-Provide* Spiritual Covenant of our Forefather, Abraham. What does He have to do with us now? This Spiritual Mindset allows us to connect to *The-LORD-Will-Provide* Promise. Blasphemy, right? Wrong!

"Then Abraham lifted his eyes and looked, and there behind him was a ram caught in a thicket by its horns. So Abraham went and took the ram, and offered it up for a burnt offering instead of his son. And Abraham called the name of the place, The-LORD-Will-Provide; as it is said to this day, 'In the Mount of the LORD it shall be provided.' Then the Angel of the LORD called to Abraham a second time out of heaven, and said: 'By Myself I have sworn, says the LORD, because you have

done this thing, and have not withheld your son, your only son—blessing I will bless you, and multiplying I will multiply your descendants as the stars of the heaven and as the sand which is on the seashore; and your descendants shall possess the gate of their enemies. In your seed all the nations of the earth shall be blessed, because you have obeyed My voice.' " Genesis 22:13-18.

Above all, we must learn how to tap into the Heart of God, allowing Him to open His Mighty Hand with Divine Provisions, Wisdom, Secrets, and Treasures. To connect from the *Hand of God* to ours, we must follow the Five Fingers of Obedience *As It Pleases Him*.

- ☐ The Pinky Finger: *"Do not withhold good from those to whom it is due, when it is in the power of your hand to do so."* Proverbs 3:27.
- ☐ The Ring Finger: *"Do not say to your neighbor, 'Go, and come back, And tomorrow I will give it,' When you have it with you."* Proverbs 3:28.
- ☐ The Middle Finger: *"Do not devise evil against your neighbor, for he dwells by you for safety's sake."* Proverbs 3:29.
- ☐ The Index Finger: *"Do not strive with a man without cause, if he has done you no harm."* Proverbs 3:30.
- ☐ The Thumb: *"Do not envy the oppressor, and choose none of his ways."* Proverbs 3:31.

The fingered countdown will work wonders on our Kingdomly Mindset and Heart Posture. What does this mean? When we are confused, at a crossroads, or do not have a Bible handy, we can open our hands, doing a countdown with these Spiritual Decrees to make better decisions, *As It*

Pleases God. Does this work? We cannot go wrong standing on the Word of God; plus, it gives us Spiritual Leverage in presenting our case, *Spirit to Spirit.*

What guarantee do we have when utilizing the *Hand of God*? Utilizing the Hand of God with *The Lord Will Provide* Mindset will usher in knowledge, wisdom, expectation, and understanding. Is this Biblical? I would have it no other way, "*Happy is the man who finds wisdom, And the man who gains understanding; For her proceeds are better than the profits of silver, And her gain than fine gold. She is more precious than rubies, And all the things you may desire cannot compare with her. Length of days is in her right hand, In her left hand riches and honor. Her ways are ways of pleasantness, And all her paths are peace. She is a tree of life to those who take hold of her, And happy are all who retain her.*" Proverbs 3:13-18.

How can we become a Tree of Life? Before becoming a Tree of Life, we must focus on sowing good seeds, developing a Godly rooting system of conveyance, Spiritually Tilling our own ground, and enduring the Spiritual Pruning Process. What if we opt out of becoming a Tree of Life? We become a Tree of Death, Mentally, Physically, Emotionally, and Spiritually, bearing all types of rotten fruits appearing good! Really? Yes, really! Ask the psyche; it will tell us most of what we need to know while lying about the rest.

How can we REVERSE ENGINEER a Tree of Death, bringing it back to life, *As It Pleases God*? Listed below are a few pointers on Spiritual Regrafting, but not limited to such:

- ☐ "*Therefore submit to God.*" James 4:7a.
- ☐ "*Resist the devil and he will flee from you.*" James 4:7b.
- ☐ "*Draw near to God and He will draw near to you.*" James 4:8a.

- ☐ *"Cleanse your hands, you sinners; and purify your hearts, you double-minded."* James 4:8b.
- ☐ Repent…*"Lament and mourn and weep! Let your laughter be turned to mourning and your joy to gloom."* James 4:9.
- ☐ *"Humble yourselves in the sight of the Lord, and He will lift you up."* James 4:10.
- ☐ *"Do not speak evil of one another, brethren. He who speaks evil of a brother and judges his brother, speaks evil of the law and judges the law. But if you judge the law, you are not a doer of the law but a judge."* James 4:11.

Why is the Spiritual Rooting System so important in the Eye of God? Simply put, *"There is one Lawgiver, who is able to save and to destroy. Who are you to judge another?"* James 4:12. If we are not appointed as Judges to enforce the Laws of the Land, then we have no right to point the finger outside of evaluating Spiritual Fruits for our own good and well-being of our seeds, roots, grafting system, or Tree of Life.

Why is it important to know the difference in judging people, places, and things? For example, if someone is dealing with anger, we do not know where the anger is derived from; therefore, we should avoid judging the person and deal with the Spirit governing the behavior. Or, we should deal with the behavior by gaining an understanding of the seed, root, and fruit without mistreating, abusing, judging anyone, or dragging someone through the mud. What is the big deal? What if God uses that to train, prepare, or redirect them? Will we be the ones to destroy or traumatize them without taking the time to educate, motivate, or encourage them with the Fruits of the Spirit and Christlike Character?

What if we need to call someone out? Calling someone out does not get us brownie points in the Eye of God, nor does it enhance our *Kingdomly Confidence*; it deflates it! We must feed God's sheep, not beat them up Mentally, Physically, Emotionally, or Spiritually. For this reason, God is looking for people skills. Why? Effective communication, *As It Pleases God*, is how to truly gain Spiritual Confidence without destroying, dismantling, or disenfranchising.

Divine Communication

In the Eye of God, communication is one of the most important skills we can develop personally, professionally, socially, and privately. It can make or break relationships, careers, and opportunities, holding us back from our Predestined Blueprint or Promises.

How should we communicate *As It Pleases God*? Please allow me to answer this question with another: 'How did Jesus communicate?' Jesus was the MASTER communicator who spoke with authority, clarity, precision, and compassion. What made Him such a MASTER?

- ☐ He knew how to CONNECT with different audiences.
- ☐ He knew how to persuade and influence.
- ☐ He knew how to teach and inspire.
- ☐ He knew how to handle conflict and criticism.
- ☐ He knew when to speak and when to listen.
- ☐ He knew when to ask questions and when to give answers.
- ☐ He knew when to use words, stories, and actions.

Jesus did not speak randomly or casually, wasting words or time. He had a clear purpose and mission for His communicative efforts, revealing God's Heavenly Character and aligning His words with His actions. He did not get distracted by trivial or irrelevant issues, wasting precious time on arguments or debates that did not matter. Nor did He compromise or dilute His Divine Message from the Heavenly of Heavens to please people; He said what he needed to say and kept it moving in the Spirit of Excellence. Listed below are a few ways Jesus confidently communicated back then, but not limited to such:

- ☐ He communicated through His teachings and parables (stories) to convey important messages, lessons, and warnings.
- ☐ He communicated through miracles and acts of healing, demonstrating His Divine Power and Compassion.
- ☐ He communicated through His example of living a humble and selfless life, inspiring us to do the same.
- ☐ He communicated through His use of metaphors and symbolisms, helping us to understand complex Spiritual Principles, Concepts, and Precepts.
- ☐ He communicated through His interactions with people from all walks of life, demonstrating His love and acceptance for all.
- ☐ He communicated through His prayers and conversations with God, showing us the importance of prayer and a deep *Spirit to Spirit* Relationship with Him.
- ☐ He communicated through His use of questions, provoking the elements of thought and encouraging us to reflect on our beliefs and actions.

- ☐ He communicated through His use of humor and wit, making His teachings more engaging and memorable.
- ☐ He communicated through His use of analogies and comparisons, helping us to understand Spiritual Truths in a more relatable way.
- ☐ He communicated through His use of repetition, emphasizing important points and messages.
- ☐ He communicated through silence, allowing us to reflect and contemplate His teachings.
- ☐ He communicated through His use of forgiveness, teaching us the importance of forgiveness, mercy, and grace.
- ☐ He communicated through His use of rebuke, correcting us when we are wrong and guiding us toward the right path.
- ☐ He communicated through His use of encouragement, inspiring us to live our lives to the fullest and reach our full potential.
- ☐ He communicated through His use of unexpected twists, challenging us to think in new and creative ways.
- ☐ He communicated through His use of prophecy, revealing God's Divine Plan for the future and giving us hope for what will come.
- ☐ He communicated through His use of miracles and signs, proving His Divine Nature and inspiring faith in those around Him.
- ☐ He communicated through His use of humility and servanthood, teaching us to put others before ourselves and serve those in need.
- ☐ He communicated through His use of love, showing us the ultimate example of the power of love and selflessness.
- ☐ He communicated through the Fruits of the Spirit.

With *The WHY Blueprint*, we have just laid out the Blueprint of Jesus that can help us gain the *Kingdom Confidence* He displayed. We are not exempt from communicating likewise or immune to developing our people skills. We have to get it together for our sake and our BLOODLINE.

What if we lack the proper etiquette or intellect? We are relational beings; therefore, this can never become our excuse in the Eye of God. Why? All we need to do is ask, do, and become, especially when dealing with the ONENESS of the Kingdom or His sheep! Furthermore, He is not looking for perfection but for WILLINGNESS and CONSISTENCY. Here is the Spiritual Seal: *"Most assuredly, I say to you, he who believes in Me, the works that I do he will do also; and greater works than these he will do, because I go to My Father. And whatever you ask in My name, that I will do, that the Father may be glorified in the Son. If you ask anything in My name, I will do it."* John 14:12-14.

How does Oneness apply to us? In the Eye of God, it is crucial to understand the difference when dealing with all things Spiritual. When building *Kingdom Confidence*, unifying as ONE is key. Why? Without ONENESS, there is division. For example, when I use the term in the Eye of God, those who do not understand the Mind of God would use the terminology Eyes of God, which indicates DIVISION. Blasphemy, right? Wrong! If we cover one eye, we will perceive what we are looking at in one way. If we cover the other eye, we will see the same thing differently with an adjusted angle. While simultaneously assuming it was the same view until we opened both eyes, we realized our peripheral view was hindered. Why would this happen? God has prewired our brains to AUTOFILL to keep us from panicking when division occurs, helping us to adapt to whatever or whomever.

The same Spiritual Autofill occurs in the Realm of the Spirit, protecting us from negative conditioning, trauma, abuse, neglect, bullying, and so on. Therefore, we must make a conscious effort to become One with the Holy Trinity, use the Fruits of the Spirit, Spiritually Till our own ground, and put on the *Whole Armor of God*, preventing the Mind, Body, and Soul from becoming divided, fighting against each other, zapping our *Kingdomly Confidence*.

Can the Mind, Body, and Soul really fight against each other? It happens all too often. The moment we find ourselves duking it out with others without cause or remorse, it indicates internal conflict. How can this cause conflict, especially when we did not initiate it? It does not matter if we are the initiator or initiatee. If we are NOT in fight or flight mode to save our lives and casually engaging in destructive behaviors 'just because' without exhibiting self-control, it indicates that our Spiritual Compass is keeled.

More importantly, NO ONE is exempt from internal conflict; it is a matter of knowing what to do, what NOT to do, and why we are doing it. If not, Hosea 4:6 becomes relevant in saying: "*My people are destroyed for lack of knowledge.*"

As relational beings, our conscience is designed to kick into high gear to resolve or defuse conflicts through repentance, forgiveness, mercifulness, and compassion. If our conscience is not working correctly, it means the psyche is out of gas. We must refuel ourselves with the Word of God, cover ourselves with the Blood of Jesus, invoke the presence of the Holy Spirit, repent, apologize, forgive, utilize the Fruits of the Spirit, give thanks for the experience, create a positive win-win, document it, and share it as a Testimony for the greater good of the Kingdom of God, continually working on our people skills. I know it sounds like a lot to do, but once we begin to use this process, it becomes a piece of cake...I PROMISE!

What are the indications of having excellent people skills? Although our level of people skills can vary, becoming a matter of perception, mindset, and exposure, God weighs the heart. What is the purpose of God weighing the heart? Because trauma speaks loudly. Unfortunately, people will put off on us how they feel about themselves, without understanding the facts or denying the truth, creating inaccurate measures. Nevertheless, listed below are a few skills designed to help polish up our communicative efforts, but not limited to such:

- ☐ **Active Listening**: The act of paying attention to what someone is saying or doing without interrupting or getting distracted.
- ☐ **Empathy**: The ability to understand, relate to, and share the feelings of others.
- ☐ **Confidence**: Being self-assured Mentally, Physically, Emotionally, and Spiritually while projecting a positive image.
- ☐ **Clear Communication**: Articulating thoughts, intents, or ideas effectively and understandably.
- ☐ **Adaptability**: Being flexible and able to adjust to different situations and sudden changes.
- ☐ **Patience**: Demonstrating a willingness to wait with a calm state of being, showing tolerance.
- ☐ **Positive Attitude**: Maintain an optimistic outlook, look for the good or the win-win, and be enthusiastic.
- ☐ **Diplomacy**: Handling situations tactfully with pristineness and sensitivity.
- ☐ **Respectfulness**: Showing consideration, reverence, and regard for others.
- ☐ **Trustworthiness**: Being reliable, faithful, and honest, operating with integrity.

- **Conflict Resolution**: Ability to handle disagreements, defuse issues, and find a mutually beneficial solution.
- **Teamwork**: The ability to work cooperatively to achieve a common goal.
- **Leadership**: Inspiring, mentoring, and guiding others to succeed in reaching their highest and best potential.
- **Problem-solving**: Identifying issues, understanding the problems, and developing solutions.
- **Creativity**: Thinking inside, outside, around, through, over, and under the box to find new solutions, leaving no stone unturned.
- **Cultural Competence**: Understanding and respecting the diversity of different backgrounds, cultures, and mentalities.
- **Emotional Intelligence**: Being aware of and managing one's own thoughts, emotions, desires, wants, needs, and those of others.
- **Humility**: Being humble and acknowledging the needs and contributions of others.
- **Approachability**: Being accessible, relatable, relevant, and easy to talk to.
- **Gratitude**: Show appreciation and express thanks for all things and the contributions of others.

In *Kingdom Communication*, our people skills are interpersonal, helping us communicate, collaborate, and connect with others in various settings, circumstances, situations, and events. When using our people skills in the workplace, we will find that they are just as effective as they would be in our personal lives. With *The WHY Blueprint*, we cover all the bases, from personal to professional, ensuring BALANCE.

What if we do not have good people skills? We can work on them daily. Still, we should not use this as an excuse not to become better, stronger, and wiser.

For example, MY SKILLS WERE DEPLORABLE when I began my Spiritual Journey. Why? I did not know any better! Really? Yes, really! I was NOT taught about having excellent people skills, effectively communicating, or using the Fruits of the Spirit; yet, above all, I was taught RESPECTFULNESS.

While operating in a charactorial deficit, I knew I needed more than respectfulness to get me across the threshold of my faith. So, I consciously decided to do better, REFUSING to be mean, nasty, rude, hateful, treat others as I was once treated, or intentionally traumatize another human being.

More importantly, I realized our parents teach us based on what they were taught or their capacity; therefore, we should not blame or hold any resentment because that was the training ground God chose for us. Either we rise above it or fall below it, period!

If we want to break the negative cycle, we must stop making excuses, vowing to learn, understand, grow, and sow back into the Kingdom, *As It Pleases God*, like I am doing now.

How do we know if we possess bad people skills? Listed below are some possible characteristics, but not limited to such:

- ☐ Difficulty making eye contact.
- ☐ Poor listening skills.
- ☐ Interrupting others while they speak.
- ☐ Talking too much about oneself.
- ☐ Failing to show empathy.
- ☐ Being insensitive to others' feelings.

- ☐ Making inappropriate comments or jokes.
- ☐ Being too critical or judgmental.
- ☐ Being rude or disrespectful.
- ☐ Being unapproachable or unfriendly.
- ☐ Being unreliable or untrustworthy.
- ☐ Failing to keep promises or commitments.
- ☐ Being defensive or argumentative.
- ☐ Being passive-aggressive.
- ☐ Avoiding conflict or difficult conversations.
- ☐ Being unable to read social cues.
- ☐ Being unaware of personal space boundaries.
- ☐ Invading others' personal space.
- ☐ Ignoring boundaries set by others.
- ☐ Failing to adapt to different social situations.

Building our people skills is optional; however, to become and remain genuinely or externally BLESSED and happy *As It Pleases God*, there are conditions. What about internally? We have the Fruits of the Spirit...there are no laws against them; we all have the free will or Spiritual Right to use or not to use them. Remember, worldly blessings (material gain) differ from Heavenly Blessings or Promises. Even if we often lump them all together, in the Eye of God, His Divine Ways are not ours. How so? He begins working on us from the inside out, and worldliness works in reverse from the outside in. According to the Beatitudes in Matthew 5:3-12, here is what we must know:

- ☐ Blessed are the poor in Spirit, for theirs is the Kingdom of Heaven.

- ☐ Blessed are those who mourn, for they shall be comforted.

- ☐ Blessed are the meek, for they shall inherit the earth.

- ☐ Blessed are those who hunger and thirst for righteousness, for they shall be filled.

- ☐ Blessed are the merciful, for they shall obtain mercy.

- ☐ Blessed are the pure in heart, for they shall see God.

- ☐ Blessed are the peacemakers, for they shall be called sons of God.

- ☐ Blessed are those who are persecuted for righteousness' sake, for theirs is the Kingdom of Heaven.

- ☐ Blessed are you when they revile and persecute you, and say all kinds of evil against you falsely for My sake.

- ☐ Rejoice and be exceedingly glad, for great is your reward in Heaven, for so they persecuted the prophets who were before you.

Most think these are rules, but they are a BLUEPRINTED GUIDE reflecting God's expectations for building *The LORD-Will-Provide* Mentality. In addition, putting on the *Whole Armor of God* with His Divine Expectations met is similar to polishing our Spiritual Armor. Really? Yes, really! He does not like dullness. Is this a little judgmental? Maybe or maybe not...I am just the Messenger. *"For the shepherds have* become dull-hearted, and have not sought the LORD; Therefore they shall not prosper, and all their flocks shall be scattered." Jeremiah 10:21.

The Contingency Clause

When operating as if there are no Spiritual Contingency Clauses, doing whatever with whomever, we cannot think we are operating at full capacity, *As It Pleases God*. How can I say such a thing, right? In putting all the fluff aside, the conscience will NOT allow it because we are Spiritual Beings having a human experience. It will send all types of red flags to the psyche, letting us know something is wrong while attempting to self-correct or regulate us.

If self-correction does not occur, we will feel a void from within, regardless of who we are, why we are, where we are from, or what our status is. For this reason, it behooves us to use the BLUEPRINTED GUIDES to help us.

What if we choose not to use our Blueprinted Guides or the Word of God? We have free will to opt in or out; however, here is what we must know: "*And in them the prophecy of Isaiah is fulfilled, which says: 'Hearing you will hear and shall not understand, And seeing you will see and not perceive; For the hearts of this people have grown dull. Their ears are hard of hearing, And their eyes they have closed, Lest they should see with their eyes and hear with their ears, Lest they should understand with their hearts and turn, So that I should heal them. But* **BLESSED** *are your eyes for they see, and your ears for they hear; for assuredly, I say to you that many prophets and righteous men desired to see what you see, and did not see it, and to hear what you hear, and did not hear it.'*" Matthew 13:14-17.

Building *The-LORD-Will-Provide* Mentality is a Spiritual Journey full of lessons, tests, insights, information, and integral moments; thus, I do not want anyone to miss out on what rightly belongs to them. How can we miss out, especially if it is ours? Unfortunately, Spiritual Blindness, Deafness, Muteness, and self-sabotage are real. If we do not know or understand our Divine Purpose, we will not know if we miss it. It is hidden in plain sight, forcing a cycle of déjà vu until we come to ourselves Mentally, Physically, Emotionally, and Spiritually.

How do we get off this merry-go-round? We must begin seeking our reason for being, one step at a time. Why? Our Predestined Blueprint demands our attention; if not, the mark of insecurity will follow us, even if we pretend we have it going on.

This book, *The WHY Blueprint* (What Hurts You is What Heals You), is a part of God's Divine Plan to push us forward into GREATNESS. Yet, in all we do, we must also incorporate this into our personal, business, or professional WHY Blueprints:

The Greatest Commandments:

1. *"And you shall love the LORD your God with all your heart, with all your soul, with all your mind, and with all your strength."* Mark 12:30.

2. *"You shall love your neighbor as yourself."* Mark 12:31.

The Golden Rule:

"Therefore, whatever you want men to do to you, do also to them, for this is the Law and the Prophets." Matthew 7:12.

The Lord's Prayer:

"*Our Father in heaven, Hallowed be Your name. Your Kingdom come. Your will be done, on earth as it is in Heaven. Give us this day our daily bread. And forgive us our debts, as we forgive our debtors. And do not lead us into temptation, but deliver us from the evil one. For Yours is the Kingdom and the power and the glory forever. Amen.*" Matthew 6:9-13.

Chapter Twelve
Doctoring The WHY

You are the EXPERT of your Predestined Blueprint, even if you do not realize it or your present moment contradicts it. However, your expertise will depend upon your ability to document, plan, and convey. Nor should you have a problem with someone asking for documented proof, or when they test your Spirit. When living at our highest and best potential, we cannot become quick to judge anyone or anything. Why should we not judge? We may not know what or who God is using, what is designed as our stepping stone, or who the diamonds in the rough are, regardless of whether we are Holy Ghost-Filled and Fire-Baptized.

Without having a *Spirit to Spirit* Connection, *As It Pleases God*, He will withhold information from us to protect them or us. If, for some reason, He knows we cannot bear it, we will be traumatized by it or them, or we will misuse the information, He will also deny access to certain people, places, and things. For this reason, we must avoid becoming our own patients, even if we have issues or they have them.

In living our best lives, *As It Pleases God*, the goal is to develop the proper MINDSET, bringing positivity to any situation, circumstance, or event. How can we usher in positivity in a negative situation? It is done by using the Fruits of the Spirit and behaving Christlike, which will cause ALL THINGS to work together for our good, even if it does not look good.

On the other hand, if we operate with rotten fruits, behaving waywardly and selfishly, without self-correction or self-control, we will begin turning on ourselves from the inside out. While at the same time, we appear highly adorned outwardly or have it all together but rotten to the core, especially behind closed doors or when no one is looking.

Listen to me, and listen well; NO ONE can doctor your soul besides you. We are all born with a Doctoring Spirit, and if you do not connect it to the Holy Spirit, you will find the psyche overruling you with your permission.

Although God has given us people to guide, mentor, and motivate us in our healing journey, we must consciously choose to take authority. Unfortunately, if we do not know this, we will return to our idolatrous doctor, chosen teacher, or the wolf in sheep's clothing, with the same recurring issues, with zero understanding and depleted faith.

Why would our doctor of choice be an idol? If they were not idolized in some way or sought to be idolized, they would have advised us to take responsibility for our actions, reactions, thoughts, beliefs, biases, and words, leading us back to God Almighty instead of allowing us to become soulishly confused.

No matter where we are, who we are, and why, soulish confusion is real, even if we do not discuss it, keeping it on the hush-hush. Why is this kept on the hush-hush? First and foremost, we do not truly understand what soulish confusion is or is not. Secondly, we cannot discuss it with anyone due to the lack of knowledge. And thirdly, we do not want people to think we are going off the deep end.

If we do not know about the soulish matters of the psyche, and they do not know, then my question is, 'Who will we call on, especially when our secret demons are haunting us?' Will we call Ghostbusters? Will we call Soul Busters, Mind Busters, or Thought Busters? Will the church kick us out if we ask for help? Will they usher us into a back room to hush our demons to avoid scaring people, or will they bodaciously shut us down to prevent us from ruining their live stream?

On the other hand, are they eager to put us on blast, exposing our hidden issues to appear better than us? Is this not why most of us avoid saying something about our secret issues? Is this not why we avoid dealing with what we do not understand?

When the truth is, we all have little hush-hush issues we are unwilling to share due to being ushered into the back room or out of the church. With all due respect, I am not targeting anyone or an establishment; I am targeting the TEMPLE from within. Outsourcing our souls without Divine Resources, *As It Pleases God*, can become a tricky situation of judgment or compounded trauma. We must involve God in our equational efforts, even if we pay a professional a hefty fee or tithing for our help.

Doctoring the WHY is imperative to extract the *Diamond in the Rough*. What makes this so important? It keeps us from lying to ourselves or depending on tangible people, places, and things to determine our worthiness. We all have a WHY... and for this reason, we push forward, push back, hold ourselves back, degrade others, or point the finger.

Whatever it causes, we are responsible, blaming no one or nothing.

The known or unknown choice of blaming no one determines the leaders, followers, dictators, game changers, and Servants of the Kingdom. What does all of this mean? For example, when someone tries to convince me of their righteousness or astuteness and does not assume responsibility for anything, I already know they are a master manipulator. How would I know this? According to the Heavenly of Heavens, as long as we have breath in our bodies, we all have something to work on or at. When we think other people are causing our issues, we have given our Spiritual Power away to please ourselves or others.

When *Doctoring our WHY*, we are always a work-in-progress because there is something to learn, glean, share, or understand. Plus, as long as the season changes, Divine Order is still at play, and we are a part of this ORDER in Earthen Vessel as ONE. Denying this fact will cause the Vicissitudes and Cycles of Life to self-correct or self-heal. The moment we begin to fight back or refuse this process, the issues of life will make an example out of us, our lives, or our Bloodline. More importantly, if we have not taken the time to unveil our reason for being or Divine Blueprint, it increases the pressure, similar to a hurricane continuing to hit a specific area with no mercy.

Unfortunately, nature is designed to level the playing field, forcing us to unite. If not, it will unmercifully continue until it gets our attention or until we become victims ourselves. To be clear, I wish the best for everyone; however, I must bring Divine Revelation, giving an opportunity to self-correct.

I have strategically placed this as the 12th chapter for a reason...To give Divine Instructions and Decrees. My ear has been to the ground for a few months now. From my Divine

Analysis, I must hang my head down in utter shame. I never thought I would see this type of underhanded mayhem and the support of staking claim to something stolen from our Forefathers. The historical lies have AWAKENED past atrocities, ensuing in a Spiritual Battle that we fail to understand. I have heeded the warning previously, and here we are again...Stirring the Waters. The Spiritual Wailing has released a SPIRITUAL SOUND to get our attention. As I stated earlier, the land is designed to heal itself, and the Wrath of God is inevitable if we fail to listen.

When dealing with all things Spiritual, we cannot play around with people, places, things, and cultures we do not understand. The Spiritual Demarcation has been set and cannot and will not change. It will fight back tooth and nail, especially when marked with a Trail of Blood, Sweat, and Tears. If one does not know about it, then it is time to get in the know.

God does not want us to be clueless about WHY this is happening or think He is unjust. He has made specific Promises to our Forefathers, and He will not have mercy on those who do not take the time to understand the Spiritual Covenants. If we want to play, it is best to play outside the Spiritual Covenants or within our own. Why? When we contend with God's Promises, He will place us in the category of trying to become a Pharaoh over His chosen elect. In time, plagues will come, shaking us to the core.

We often think the story of the Children of Israel and Pharaoh is a fairytale, but we are living it right now. How can we possibly take back what does not belong to us in the first place? All things belong to God, placing us as stewards with Spiritual Dominion. And if we violate the DOMAIN of a Spiritual Dominion set forth by God Almighty, we will have issues. Therefore, if we are not up-to-date on our historical edifices, we will 'get got' for what we do not know.

How can we 'get got' by what we do not know? Anything or anyone marked with a trail of blood, sweat, and tears with the Holy Trinity involved, BEWARE! When we play dirty with Spiritual Covenants, Marks, Territories, the same Spirit taunting King Saul for his disobedience will seek us out. Why? We cannot DISRESPECT what is SACRED.

For example, when speaking our Spiritual Language or Spiritual Tongue, we must exhibit RESPECT to the hearer or the doer. Why? When speaking in tongues, it should be done with the presence of the Holy Spirit within us, not the atmosphere. Once again, it is when the Holy Spirit comes UPON you. Not around you, but UPON you.

And now, for some odd reason, we have allowed speaking tongues to go to our heads, and we just let it all hang out. What does this mean? Most of the tongues we speak are NOT of God. I will say it again; it is NOT of God, PERIOD! Who am I to judge, right? Absolutely, no judgment intended, but I am going to tell the truth about this mockery taking place from the pulpit to the Four Corners.

Should we not speak in our Heavenly Language? Of course, we should, but within the Holy Constraints of it, such as publicly with an interpreter, in worshiping our Heavenly Father, or in our prayer closet in our *Spirit to Spirit* Relations. The one-on-one prophesying, manipulating others with tongues, or using tongues as a filler without an interpreter is highly frowned upon by our Heavenly Father. We need to stop playing with God like this...

For example, as a Spiritual Elite, and someone walks up to me speaking in tongues, I will rebuke them and the Spirit they came with, while not saying one word to them. Why would I rebuke them? First, they were not operating with the Holy Spirit because He would have warned them that I would not play around with this type of foolery. Secondly, if they do not know what they are saying or who they are dealing with, how could they possibly know which Spirit is operating? Thirdly, the Holy Spirit is RESPECTFUL. He knows I do not play like this, and He would not try me in such a manner. He will approach me with what I understand, allowing me to test the Spirit and Fruits of what I am dealing with. For this reason, I will speak to the Deceptive Spirit, shutting them down without uttering a mumbling word to the hearer.

Doctoring the WHY of your life can make you Sacred in the Eye of God. How? When operating in Purpose on purpose, we place ourselves under the watchful Eye of God. Simply put, if it is from God, He will protect what and who belongs to Him. On the other hand, if we do our own thing, only including Him on the backend, then He is not obligated to protect us, it, or them.

When building a Spiritual Blueprint, be it personal, private, or business-related, it behooves us to include God Almighty, add much RESPECT, and immerse ourselves in outright humility using the Fruits of the Spirit and behaving Christlike. What can this do for us? It BLESSES our hands, causing all things to work for our good. Instead of inadvertently plaguing them, invoking things to work against us.

Beyond all measures, *What Hurts You is What Heals You!* The *WHY Blueprint* and *Doctoring the WHY* are what you need for such a time as this. To become the EXPERT in your life, you must learn from everyone, anyone, or anything without limiting yourself. Remember, the medicine or salve is already within; use them and grow GREAT.

Dr. Y. Bur

www.ingramcontent.com/pod-product-compliance
Lightning Source LLC
Chambersburg PA
CBHW071712160426
43195CB00012B/1657